My Greatest Fight

40 BOXERS DESCRIBE
MY GREATEST FIGHT

KEN GORMAN

MAINSTREAM
PUBLISHING
EDINBURGH AND LONDON

To the memory of Steve Watt, Bradley Stone and James Murray. And to fighters everywhere: The Bravest of Brave Men.

First published in Great Britain in 1996 by
MAINSTREAM PUBLISHING COMPANY (EDINBURGH) LTD
7 Albany Street
Edinburgh EH1 3UG

ISBN 1 85158 844 2

A catalogue record for this book is available from the British Library

Typeset in Sabon
Printed and bound in Great Britain by Butler and Tanner Ltd, Frome

Contents

Acknowledgements

To the boxers who gave up their valuable time to help me compile this work, I offer my grateful thanks. No book is complete without its pictures. I would like to express my particular thanks to Lawrence Lustig, Sports Photographer of the Daily Star, for his splendid work on both the front and back covers of the jacket. I also thank the Daily Star and the Sunday Mirror for supplying the pictures inside. And thanks, as well, to Reg Gutteridge, doyen of television ringside commentators, for his help and encouragement.

The Lion of Africa

Muhammad Ali v George Foreman

Muhammad Ali, formerly Cassius Clay, was born in Louisville, Kentucky, on 17 January 1942. As an 18-year-old he won the gold medal in the light heavyweight division at the Olympic Games in Rome in 1960. He turned professional the following year to embark on an astonishing career that spanned two decades before he finally retired in 1981. In that time he fought no fewer than 25 world heavyweight title contests, becoming the first man to lose and regain the title twice.

IF MUHAMMAD ALI'S LIFE was ever penned as a work of fiction, the writer would have been scorned. Even in a sport richer than any other for the often outrageous, at times seedy and occasionally downright crazy characters it has spawned over a hundred years, Ali stands unique. There never was anyone quite like him before and it is doubtful whether we shall ever witness his like again. As a boxer he was superb, first as Cassius Clay, the brash, upstart Louisville Lip who bragged to the world what he was going to do, then went out and did it. Clay was the fastest, most nimble heavyweight of them all, his 6ft 3ins, 16 stone frame being blessed with the mobility of a middleweight. Then came his conversion from Christian to Black Muslim, his name change to Muhammad Ali and his eventual banning from the ring for three years after he refused to enlist in the US Army to fight in Vietnam. The man who returned to regain his world title was a different fighting machine. The waist had thickened, the legs no longer danced, the hands no longer pumped like pistons. But his heart, if anything, was stronger, the desire even greater, his brain endowed with the wisdom of maturity – and his body with its strength.

Physically and mentally he was a colossus as he regained the title which had been stripped from him during his enforced absence, held it for four years before losing it again, then reclaimed it once more. But even such heroic deeds are only part of the Ali legend. The world laughed at the young Clay with his manic manner, his poems, his predictions; his own countrymen reviled him for his religious convictions and his stance against the war in Vietnam; that turned to reverence as they saluted the courage way beyond the call of any earthly duty shown by the man many had branded a coward; the rest of the world, and Britain in particular, just loved him for the fun he brought along with his incredible exploits in the ring.

At his peak he was without question the most famous man on earth. That makes it all the more difficult to come to terms with the Ali of today, a figure reduced by Parkinson's syndrome – and, it must be admitted, the ravages of too many fights – to a shuffling shadow of the athlete of such sublime skills. But, thankfully, his mind remains alert. He can still recall the epic memories of great days, wondrous performances; so many it is difficult, even for him, to single out just one as the greatest of The Greatest. It could have been his first meeting with the menacing Sonny Liston, way back in 1964, when the young Clay first won the world heavyweight title from the man-monster most thought would destroy him. It could have been his third and final meeting with Joe Frazier, the first man to beat him four years earlier but battered into submission after 14 rounds of unbridled brutality in the Thriller in Manila in 1975. Perhaps the most perfect performance of his career was his three-round destruction of Cleveland Williams in 1966, when he took on a noted puncher and knocked him down four times, ending the devastation with a flurry of punches thrown with such blinding hand speed that it needed a slow motion television replay to see them land.

But if you ask Ali to name one exalted peak, one memory to cherish above all others, he answers: 'Zaire . . . I beat George Foreman, won my world title back. And in AFRICA . . .' It was the setting as much as the stakes, the sense of history as much as the achievement, which made that magical night – or rather early morning – so special to him. The Rumble in the Jungle he labelled it when the contest was made. It turned out to be the most amazing fight in heavyweight history, a night when a man seemed to dig into his soul for his strength and his inspiration.

Ali's already remarkable career had seemed to be drifting towards its inevitable conclusion when he returned after his ban to be beaten first by Frazier and then by Ken Norton – a defeat that appeared to have finally silenced the famous Lip as his jaw was broken and had to be wired together. But the mouth was back in full-throttled action as he returned to outpoint Norton in a desperately close return contest, then gain a similar revenge over Frazier. Now he was right back in the heavyweight world title picture. But to regain it would mean facing a champion who had already launched a reign of terror on all who stood, trembling, before him – and who, the experts said, had the weaponry to rule for a decade.

George Foreman was 26, six years younger than Ali, and at the awesome peak of his career. He had plundered the title by obliterating Frazier, sending him into orbit with one mighty uppercut. He had wreaked a similar trail of devastation with his 39 other opponents: only three had managed to survive, let alone challenge him. Even the tough, durable Ken Norton, who had given Ali so much trouble, could not last two rounds against Foreman's onslaught. But Ali was insistent that he could triumph against all the odds. 'I want my title back,' he said. 'When I was the champion before, I was too young to understand what it meant. Now I want it, more than anything I ever wanted in my life.'

A hustling new black promoter called Don King wanted it just as badly. King had been released from prison only three years previously after serving four years for manslaughter, but he had already spotted the world-wide appeal of Ali and the enormous global revenue from a challenge to Foreman. King had also heard that African gold could be his trump card. President Mobutu of Zaire was eager to make his mark on the world stage – and was willing to spend up to $10 million to bring the fight to his country. King guaranteed both Foreman and Ali more than $5 million each – twice the fortune any boxer had ever been paid before for one contest – to persuade them to meet on a continent where no world heavyweight title fight had ever been held before. A major American closed circuit company called Video Techniques, who would beam it round the world, were the actual promoters, but it was King's relentless energy and ability to paper over all cracks which made it happen.

The date was set for 25 September 1974 at three o'clock in the morning – an unearthly hour that would coincide with mid-evening in America, where it was to be shown on cinema screens across the country. Ali was first to arrive, some three weeks before the scheduled date – and he immediately launched a carefully orchestrated public relations campaign which would win the whole country over to his side. 'I used to think Africans were savages,' he told his hosts, 'but now that I'm here I've learned that many Africans are wiser than we are. It's great to be in a country operated by black people.' He would hammer that theme every time he was in public – and he made a point of meeting the people everywhere, even in the shanty towns around the capital, Kinshasa. Having handed out the plaudits, he would then belittle Foreman: 'He's nothing but a slow-moving Mummy . . . George hits hard, but power don't mean nothing if you got nobody to hit . . . Foreman ain't nothing, just a big bully from Texas who used to beat up people in the street . . . He don't stand a chance – when I've finished with him, he'll have so many nicks and cuts he'll look like he had a bad shave!'

Ali, like some presidential candidate eager to win the battle for the people's hearts and minds, did not resist a single opportunity to go out on the road – or even, at times, the jungle tracks – to meet them. Foreman, by contrast, remained locked in his quarters, a hostile, surly champion whose whole demeanour showed he didn't want to be there. And then, just eight days before the scheduled date, it seemed Foreman might get his way – in the most unfortunate of circumstances. He suffered a cut over his right eye in sparring when an opponent's elbow accidentally crashed into his face. It was impossible for the injury to be healed in time – and Foreman was ready to pack his bags and get the hell out of Africa and back home to Texas.

But the President had other ideas. He had invested millions in staging the fight and he was not going to see his dream evaporate now. Both Ali and Foreman were proffered 'friendly' advice by government officials that it would be 'unwise' to try to leave the country. So they stayed another five weeks until the new date, 30 October at four a.m. It was a delay that certainly worked in the challenger's favour. While Ali continued to keep busy with his roadshow, Foreman was left to brood about the cut, about the food, the water . . .

However, the champion remained an overwhelming favourite to retain his crown as fight morning finally arrived. Even the mood in Ali's own camp was one of nervous apprehension. He noticed it in his dressing-room and grinned: 'Do I look scared? This is just another day in the dramatic life of Muhammad Ali.' Sixty thousand supporters in the spruced-up, freshly painted outdoor stadium showed their emotions as they gave him a tumultuous reception – Ali had handsomely accomplished his propaganda victory. 'Ali Bomaye!' (Ali, Kill Him!) they yelled as the two fighters came together in the ring for final instructions.

In the opening round he had the crowd roaring with excitement as he stung Foreman with a sharp right, then peppered the champion's face with his jab and used his still sprightly legs to keep out of trouble. Ali's round – but he was concerned as he went back to his corner. 'The ring was so slow. Dancing all night, my legs would have got tired,' he said. The ring was brand new, but the foam rubber padding had been laid too early the previous day. In the 85-degree heat it had become soft and mushy. 'I could never have gone on like that for 15 rounds, so I knew I had to readjust my tactics.'

Thus was born the astonishing tactic to be labelled later as rope-a-dope. From early in the second round, Ali retreated to the ring ropes – and stayed there, inviting the world's most ferocious puncher to hit him as hard and as often as he could. For six tortuous rounds he stood there, his back leaning on the top rope, his feet barely moving, soaking up the unbridled punishment meted out by a champion who must have believed he was back in the gym, smashing a human punch-bag. The crowd in the stadium and cinema audiences the world over winced at the gruesome spectacle they were watching. Boxing can be brutal – but this was barbaric. This was a man too brave, too foolhardy, for his own good, and whose common sense had deserted him. This was a man who seemed hell-bent on committing suicide in the ring.

But the punches continued to rain in and the challenger, unbelievably, continued to withstand them. And gradually, as the watching world grew even more open-mouthed, those punches began to lose their power. Foreman's mighty arms were beginning to grow weary. The champion was punching himself out. 'I hit him with the hardest shots I ever threw in my life. Anyone else in the world would have crumbled. He cringed – I could see the pain in his eyes. But he wouldn't go down – and I got burned out,' Foreman was to admit later.

Even Ali confessed: 'He shook me up a few times with his right hand.' But he claimed: 'I blocked and deflected a lot of his punches, stopped them landing with their full power. After a few rounds those punches got slower, didn't hurt so much. That's when I started talking to him: "Hey, George, you can hit harder than that! I thought you were supposed to be real bad!"' Foreman must have felt by the middle stages of the scheduled 15 rounds that he was fighting a man possessed by demons. This was Africa and Ali had witchcraft on his side.

The challenger may have been on the ropes, but it was Foreman who must have felt trapped as he came out wearily for the eighth round. For two and a half minutes, like the half dozen rounds before, Ali retreated to his now-familiar haunt and Foreman trundled slowly after him. He pummelled away again, but by now those punches had lost so much of their sting that they seemed to be thrown in slow motion. Ali sensed this was the moment, this was the time to reach out for his destiny, this was the opportunity to show that whole, disbelieving world that he was still The Greatest.

Ali threw out a couple of jabs, then caught Foreman with a sharp right hand . . . and then another as the champion, his strength and energy almost drained, suddenly went backwards for the first time in the contest. Ali, like a lion sensing the kill against a wounded, exhausted buffalo, was roaring now, suddenly springing into full-blooded action. He chased after Foreman and landed another mighty right hand to send the champion crumbling to the floor. There were less than ten seconds to go in the round, and the bell tolled with two seconds of the count remaining and Foreman still trying, without success, to haul himself up. There was no strength left in the champion's legs – and maybe no more desire left in a broken heart. By the time he finally managed to lift himself to his feet, the count was over, he was knocked out – and Africa, the land of Muhammad Ali's forefathers, was saluting a new world champion.

Ten years after he had first stunned the world by defeating Sonny Liston, seven years after he had been stripped of the title, the king was on his rightful throne again. Such was the adulation heaped upon him, even from those who once saw him as the enemy, that two months later he was at the White House in Washington to meet President Gerald Ford. Only in the script Muhammad Ali penned for his life would such a scenario have been possible. No mere fiction writer could ever have dreamed it up.

Fair Dinkum for the Pom

Dennis Andries v Jeff Harding

Dennis Andries was born in Georgetown, Guyana, on 5 November 1953. He emigrated to Britain with his parents when he was a small child and settled with his family in Hackney, London, where he still lives. After a fairly undistinguished amateur career he turned professional in 1978, winning the British light heavyweight title six years later. He won the WBC world title for the first time in 1986, outpointing American J.B. Williamson in London. He lost the crown twice but regained it both times, becoming the first British fighter to win the same title three times.

EVEN SYLVESTER STALLONE, in his wildest movie dreams, could never have conjured any *Rocky* fiction to equal the real-life story of Dennis Andries. When the quiet man from Guyana travelled to Melbourne to challenge Australian Jeff Harding for the WBC world light heavyweight title on 28 July 1990, he was bidding for a unique place in boxing's hall of fame. Victory would make Andries, domiciled in London's East End at Hackney, the first British fighter ever to win the same world title three times. He had already been written off by most of the rest of the world, but that was nothing new to a warrior who had made a habit of making mugs out of all of us who thought he was too old to continue defying history and, frankly, too ordinary to gain revenge on an opponent who had knocked him into oblivion 13 months earlier. Harding was 12 years younger, was still unbeaten and was defending his title before his own volatile supporters on the other side of the world.

The brash young man from Sydney had goaded Andries at their press conference, telling him, 'I knocked you out once and I'm gonna do it again – only it'll be easier this time.' The rest of Australia thought likewise. British boxing was not held in particularly high esteem over there at the time. Only a few months previously another British veteran and long-time foe of Andries, Tom Collins, had gone to Brisbane and quit on his stool after just two rounds, unwilling to endure any further punishment from Harding's powerful fists.

Andries seemed nothing more than another ancient sacrificial offering from the mother country. 'I kept hearing this crap from everybody over there, they were saying things like "Our guy will knock you out nice and quick, then you can go home and take tea with the Queen!" But you know what? The more they said it, the more determined I got. Man, I hate it when people don't show me no respect. Every fighter deserves respect, we're all brave men. All those guys laughing at me really got me mad.'

Andries was pushing 37 by this time and he had already been a professional fighter for 12 years. There had been no short-cut to the top for him. He had come up the hard way, fighting many of his contests in his opponents' back yards, often at a couple of days' notice – occasionally only at a few hours' notice. He was already into his 33rd year when he won the world title for the first time, outgaming and outpointing J.B. Williamson in London. Such was his low-key attitude to success that he came to the press conference in the West End the following morning on a tube train – carrying the prized WBC belt in a brown paper bag!

'I never was one for celebrating – it was just a job to be done and I done it,' he said. He wasn't too proud, either, to gamble his whole future when he lost the title to Tommy Hearns in Detroit in March 1987. Hearns, the famed and feared Hit-Man from America's Motor City, had knocked Andries down seven times. But each time he fell, Dennis climbed doggedly back to his feet before the slaughter was mercifully stopped. The very next morning, Andries asked Hearns's legendary manager and trainer Emmanuel Steward if he could join their team! 'I figure that if a guy is good enough to beat you, he must have things you can learn about. Emmanuel had a great name as a trainer, so I figured that the only way for me to get better was to learn from him,' said Andries. Steward, initially stunned at the notion, eventually agreed to let Andries spend some time at his fabled Kronk Gym. 'I admire his determination. I knew the guy had balls, the way he kept getting up against Tommy. So I put him in with some real tough guys at the gym, just to see if he could take it, day after day,' said Steward.

Andries spent months away from his family, living in an apartment across the road from the gym, which is set in one of the toughest areas of one of America's truly tough cities. 'In the end I got respect in the gym and on the street,' recalls Andries. 'They didn't like the idea of this Limey guy in the place, so I had some real brutal wars in the gym. As tough as any fight you care to mention. I had to break so many noses and bust so many ribs in that gym before they accepted me. That set me up for anything. I lived like a monk, running, training, then back to the apartment to eat and sleep. I was always a strong man, but I got stronger every day. And when people used to make jokes about my age, that annoyed me. You're as old as you want to be in this life. I knew I was as fit as anybody.'

When Hearns gave up the title, Andries was nominated to face unbeaten American Tony Willis for the vacant crown in Tucson, Arizona, in February 1989. Willis, a loose-limbed and hard-punching prospect, was a red-hot favourite but Andries, with Steward in his corner, showed his immense physical and mental strength to bulldoze through his opponent and wear down his resistance. By the fifth round Willis could offer nothing more – and the title belonged to Andries again.

Not for long, though. Four months later it seemed that his age had finally caught up with him as he was pummelled into a last-round stoppage by the rough, tough Harding in Atlantic City. I remember asking Andries the following morning: 'Is it time to quit?' He gave me an old-fashioned stare. 'I want that title back, I ain't walking away now,' he answered. And if that meant having to travel to the other side of the world, so be it.

That is why he was here in Melbourne, him and his tiny entourage, to seek his day of vengeance. 'There were just six of us, including me and Manny Steward. Then John Morris, the secretary of the British Boxing Board, turned up a few days before the fight to support me. That gave us a title – the Magnificent Seven!' grinned Andries. 'They had to face a whole lot of bad guys, but you know they triumphed. I just knew we were going to do the same.

'I don't make excuses, but I just couldn't make the weight when I fought Harding the first time. That's why I died in the later rounds. But this time I had worked harder than I ever had before. I was in superb condition. My plan was to make him work and work, right from the first bell. I knew he was a tough kid, a charging rhino I used to call him. But I would take the sting from him, I would wear him down.'

Harding was brimful of confidence, bordering on brashness, as the fight began. And he seemed to be in control in the early rounds, peppering Andries's face with his hard punches. But if the challenger was hurt he never showed it, he never blinked. 'I wanted that title so bad that I just refused to be denied,' he said. 'And I could sense as the rounds went by, that he didn't have my fitness or my stamina. He was already beginning to blow a bit. That was music to me. I knew he was mine.' As Andries began to power his way into the fight, the baying crowd became much quieter. Suddenly it was Harding who was being driven backwards, and it was the old man from the old country who was beginning to dictate the fight.

But Andries's growing excitement almost brought disaster in the sixth round – when he went out without his gumshield! 'It was one of those crazy things. The corner were so engrossed in the tactics for the round, we all forgot about the gumshield. I didn't even realise I wasn't wearing it until he hit me on the lip – and it banged against my teeth and started to bleed. I said to myself "Hey, you gotta be careful, otherwise you'll lose some teeth". I just had to concentrate on keeping the fight at long range, keep out of trouble.'

Those three minutes of sudden anxiety were to be followed by the ecstasy of triumph. In round seven, with Harding clearly wilting, Andries caught him with a left jab, then threw his big right hand. 'As I did, though, I got caught off balance a bit. I had to lunge with the right hand in the end – and that did the trick. I hit him high on the side of his head, near the temple. There was plenty of power there. And that spot near the temple, if you catch it right, can knock the sense clean out of an opponent.' It certainly did in this case as Harding, his brain no longer working in unison with his legs, sank to the floor and just couldn't get up. He was counted out – and Andries, unheralded, untrumpeted and, in truth, written off by all bar that faithful few, was the champion again.

For Manny Steward and the rest of his team, the celebration party went on long into the night. When they eventually staggered up to their rooms, there was the new champion sat with his coat on and his bags packed. 'I just couldn't wait to get away. I wanted to get home, see my wife and my kids. Partying ain't for me. As I said before, I just went there to do a job. And I done it. That was pleasure enough for me.'

The Warrior King

Nigel Benn v Gerald McClellan

Nigel Benn was born in Ilford, Essex, on 22 January 1964. He began boxing during his army service – he reached the rank of corporal in the Northumberland Fusiliers – and won the ABA middleweight title in 1986. He began his professional career on 28 January 1987 – six days after his 23rd birthday – and went on to win the Commonwealth middleweight title, the WBO world middleweight title and then, moving up a division, the WBC world super middleweight title.

NIGEL BENN, with masterly understatement, says, 'I guess I'm a guy who just loves a tear-up.' No British fighter of modern times ever went to war as often as this former soldier, who learned to use his fists as well as his rifle as a corporal in the Northumberland Fusiliers. It's no surprise that his ring idol was Marvin Hagler. For, like the legendary American, Benn avoided no champion, no challenger. And if they came to fight, so much the better. 'When I fight big punchers, big names, I'm scared. And when I fight through fear I'm at my best,' was his battle cry.

None came to face him boasting more of a terrifying portfolio than Gerald McClellan. The American, from Freeport, Illinois, had well earned his reputation as the most ferocious punching-machine in the world by blitzing all bar two of his 31 victims to early defeat – 20 of them in the first round. He had plundered the WBC world middleweight title by outpunching the fearsome Julian Jackson in five rounds of mayhem and had blasted Jackson to defeat inside a round of their rematch. He was moving up a division to challenge for Benn's WBC world super middleweight crown, but that left him distinctly unmoved. 'I'll be even stronger, more powerful, for the extra eight pounds. In the ring I'm an animal, I have a one-track mind – seek and destroy!' he taunted.

Their showdown was arranged for 25 February 1995, at the London Arena. And even Benn was acutely aware of the awesome threat he faced. Benn, as volatile and temperamental outside the ring as he was explosive inside those ropes, had fallen out with his promoters Frank Warren and Don King. 'I know this guy McClellan has been sent over here to bash me up, to give me a lesson because I won't be nobody's puppet,' he said. 'Life's a bitch sometimes, but I've fought Barkley, De Witt, Logan and Eubank. These are the sort of guys that put the fear of God in me, but that made me fight.'

Benn was indeed battle-hardened by brutal encounters with the likes of Iran Barkley, Doug De Witt, Anthony Logan and, his eternal enemy, Chris Eubank. So many fights developed into trench warfare that he had taken over Barry McGuigan's mantle as the most exciting, swashbuckling British fighter of his day. His first manager, Ambrose Mendy, had coined his nickname, The Dark Destroyer, and it had been well earned. But he was past his 31st birthday now, facing an opponent four years younger. Would age finally catch up with him?

'What people forgot,' he said, 'was that I was a more controlled fighter now. I'd learned to hang around. McClellan hadn't. If a fighter overwhelms opponents early, he thinks life is easy. I made the same mistake against Michael Watson [the first man to beat him, six years previously]. He covers up and survives while I blow up. Then Michael kicked my ass. I learned more in that fight than 20 previous ones. I think the same thing happened to McClellan.' Benn had also picked his way through a succession of trainers during the eight years since he had launched his professional career, but it was Jimmy Tibbs who had instilled in him the basic virtue of moving your head to avoid the full impact of blows suffered. Tibbs had left his corner by this stage, but his simple lesson was something Benn never allowed himself to forget.

Not that any words of advice or encouragement seemed of the remotest significance in the very first round, when Benn suffered such a sustained beating he was knocked clean through the ropes and out of the ring! He landed almost in the lap of ITV's ringside interviewer Gary Newbon, his feet the only part of him left in the ring as they dangled on the middle rope. Somehow he managed to extricate himself from the confusion and clamber back to beat the count. Many of the capacity 12,000 crowd must have wished he hadn't, as McClellan, sensing another early finish, battered him remorselessly.

French referee Alfred Azaro, who had never officiated at such a level before, allowed the slaughter to continue, with Benn already in such dire distress he could not throw a single punch of his own in resistance. It was as savage a beating as I have ever witnessed. But Benn shook his head defiantly as he walked back to his corner at the bell. 'I knew that at some time in the fight I was going down. I'd prepared for it. I also knew that I'd get up. I kept telling myself this over and over again at my training camp in Tenerife,' he said.

McClellan must have sensed already that he was facing a champion of remarkable courage. But it was merely a foretaste of the sheer bloody-minded defiance Benn was to produce in the succeeding rounds. The American would launch into blistering attacks, he would have Benn stumbling and scrambling like some drunk on the street. Yet time after time, just when it seemed that the destruction wreaked upon him would finally force his surrender, back he would come again, with a wild-eyed, arms-swinging counter-attack of his own. As the crowd screamed encouragement, McClellan could not have believed the evidence in front of him. Here was a victim who simply would not lie down. And perhaps the chilling realisation began to dawn on the American in the eighth round. Another merciless barrage finally saw Benn sink slowly to his knees, a combination of pain and sheer exhaustion seeming to have drained the resistance from him. He managed to raise himself back on to those tired, trembling legs as the count reached eight, but a more experienced referee than Monsieur Azaro would surely have stepped in at that juncture to save a brave man from further punishment.

But as he hesitated, Benn shook a semblance of sense back into his head, looked across the ring at his tormentor – and then leapt at him, to hit him with a stinging right hook. McClellan, whose nose appeared to be broken, was already being forced to push out his gumshield to breathe through his mouth. By the end of that astonishing eighth round he was beginning to look in acute distress himself, constantly brushing the left side of his forehead with his glove, as if frightened of some wound near his eye. After one minute 46 seconds of the tenth round, he sank slowly to one knee, remaining there as he was counted out.

21

Benn, like nearly everyone else, was totally unaware of the seriousness of McClellan's injury. The champion leapt into the air with joy, the huge crowd celebrating noisily with him. It had been a night of heroism. Now it was to turn into an aftermath of tragedy. McClellan sprawled on the ring canvas for several minutes, his back and head supported by the ropes. It seemed he was drained, physically and emotionally. Then it became obvious that his condition was far more grave as he lapsed into unconsciousness. For fully 13 minutes he lay in the corner of the ring, with anaesthetist Alistair Skelly, assisted by three other doctors, working desperately to revive him. He was eventually lifted on to a stretcher and taken to hospital, where surgeons removed a blood clot from his brain.

For days he hovered between life and death, his family brought from their home in America to be by his side. Thankfully, the skill of the medical staff saved him and he was eventually allowed to return to his own country. But it was more than four months before he was able to live in his own home again. He was severely restricted in his sight and still suffered brain damage. Benn himself had been taken to hospital after his triumph, but his powers of recovery amazed doctors to such a degree that they decided, after a thorough examination, that he was well enough to return home.

'When I got to hear about Gerald McClellan I just felt sick. Boxing's a brutal game, everybody who goes into the ring knows that,' he said. 'But this – you wish to God it had never happened. A lot of people thought it would be me lying in a hospital bed. Apart from my family, my manager Peter DeFreitas and my trainer Kevin Sanders, just about the whole world had written me off.' Only when the challenger had won his fight for life could Benn enjoy any kind of celebration. 'I feel a kind of contentment I never felt before,' he said. 'I feel I have fulfilled myself with that performance. All I can pray now is that Gerald McClellan gets better.'

The British Boxing Board of Control, rightly concerned for Benn's well-being, prevented him from fighting again for four months. He returned to successfully defend his precious world title twice more in contests that, thankfully, were not overly taxing before eventually losing a points decision to South African Sugar Boy Malinga, an old foe he had narrowly beaten four years previously. Malinga's night of revenge came just over a year after Benn's epic display against McClellan. And while the veteran Zulu from Natal was entitled to his celebration, Benn was little more than a shadow of his old self. How much of the Dark Destroyer had been left in the ring on that fateful night, how heavy the price he had to pay for his unquenchable spirit, is something we will never know. But the British sporting public will never forget him for it.

Gumfight at the KO Corral

Michael Bentt v Tommy Morrison

*Michael Bentt was born in East Dulwich, London, on 4 September
1965. His family emigrated to Jamaica when he was six years old and
moved on to New York eight years later. He had a brilliant amateur
career, becoming the first heavyweight to win three national titles in
America – he won five all told. He was also the New York Golden
Gloves champion for four years. Bentt maintained dual British and
American citizenship and boxed for England's amateur team. As a
professional he had only 13 contests before being forced to retire
through a brain disorder, but even in that short career he still won the
WBO world heavyweight title.*

FEW PUNCHES IN HISTORY have been as stunningly costly as the
right hand Michael Bentt launched at Tommy Morrison in Tulsa,
Oklahoma, on 29 October 1993. As well as obliterating Morrison's
hold on the WBO world heavyweight title, it wrecked a ten-million-
pound showdown for the Kansas City cowboy with reigning WBC
world champion, Lennox Lewis. That tasty little dish had already
been carefully prepared for Las Vegas the following spring, with
each champion earning five million pounds. But Morrison insisted,
against the advice of most of those around him, that he needed a
warm-up to help him prepare to face the dynamic Lewis. As
decisions go, it must rank with Custer's order to chase the Sioux
Indians into the Little Big Horn.

Maybe Tommy's background should have warned him of the
dangers of ambush. His mother was an Indian and his great-uncle,

so legend has it, was none other than the biggest Hollywood Indian fighter of them all, John Wayne (whose real name was Marion Morrison). But before he had outmanoeuvred and outpointed the ancient George Foreman to win his title four months earlier, Morrison – like Wayne, nicknamed The Duke – had become a movie celebrity in his own right. He starred alongside Sylvester Stallone in the last Rocky film. His problem was that in the real-life drama about to unfold at the Tulsa Convention Center Bentt decided to tear up the script and write his own.

Bentt, born in the London suburb of East Dulwich, was an engaging and remarkable character in his own right. He moved with his family to Jamaica when he was just six years old. He had already learned the rudiments of boxing by the time the family moved on to America eight years later. They settled in the Queens district of New York and Bent (by that time the family had dropped the second 't' in their surname) went on to become an outstanding amateur. He won the American national heavyweight title an astonishing five times – not even the greatest fighters before him had achieved more than two successes. He was also New York Golden Gloves champion four times. But his dream of fighting in the 1986 Olympics in Seoul was ended when Ray Mercer beat him in the American trials – and went on to take the gold medal himself.

Bent – who always insisted on keeping his British passport as well as his American one, giving him dual citizenship – was still a warm prospect when he turned professional in 1989. But he was foolishly matched in his first paid contest against Jerry Jones, a noted puncher – and a southpaw, a fact Michael did not even know until the first bell. 'I didn't know how the hell to fight him,' he admits. And as he floundered his way into his new career disaster struck as he was knocked out in the very first round.

Boxing is a cruel, unforgiving business. On the evidence of one flawed night, his career was written off by many shrewd judges. There is no finer judge of boxing flesh in England than Mickey Duff and probably no American with a keener eye for talent than Emmanuel Steward, controller of Detroit's famed Kronk Gym, but both men decided Bent suffered from what the trade calls a glass jaw or a china chin . . . that he could not take a punch without wilting. Michael himself believed his career was over before it had barely started. He walked away from the ring for 18 months, before eventually finding a man who believed in him.

New Yorker Stan Hoffman had made his fortune in the music

business, and now he enjoyed the sweat and the drama of the fight game. He had already proved himself the patron saint of lost causes, resurrecting the career of fallen champion Iran Barkley to such a dramatic degree that his charge went to Las Vegas and plundered the WBA world light heavyweight crown from Tommy Hearns. Now, after a chance meeting with Bent, he believed he had unearthed the raw material to produce another miracle. He coaxed the confidence back into Bent. And he brought in former world light heavyweight champion Eddie Mustafa Muhammad as his trainer, to rebuild his fitness and rekindle his desire. The combination worked and Bent had won ten fights in a row since his disastrous debut when the chance came to face Morrison. 'The point about it was that all people remembered about me was the first fight,' says Michael. 'You get knocked out and you get labelled as a guy with a glass jaw all your life. I knew it was crazy; I knew how well I'd been fighting. But my fights had been well away from the big venues and the television cameras. Most of the world had forgotten I existed before I got the call to fight Tommy.'

By this stage the second 't' had been added to Bentt's name again. 'When I discovered that was how it was spelt when I was born, I wanted it back. I was so proud of my British roots, right down to my right name,' he said. But Morrison did not seem over-concerned how his opponent spelt his name as the pair met for the ritual pre-fight conference. 'He just seemed to ignore me. It was an arrogance which I built up in my mind and used to my advantage,' said Bentt. 'Tommy's a nice guy, but this time he wasn't so nice. That was great. If he was gonna be careless, that made me very happy.'

Bentt had also decided on his shock tactics to draw the sting from a crowd he knew would be hostile towards him. When he entered the ring he was chewing bubble-gum – and blowing enormous bubbles! 'It was an old trick I learned from watching Michael Jordan on the basketball court,' he explained. 'He used to do it to show his opponents how relaxed and confident he was. I did the same thing. And when Tommy got into the ring after me, I chewed and blew bubbles even more furiously. I wanted him to be wary of me – boxing's so much about psychology, about getting one over on the other guy mentally. That was my plan.'

Bentt, a devout Muslim, once told me that, even in a boxing ring, he would never throw the first punch. 'That's something my religion preaches and I can never go against it,' he insisted. On this particular night, it seemed for a terrible few early seconds that he was not destined to throw a punch at all. Morrison came crouching forward, throwing a few left jabs and then a ferocious left hook – his potent weapon – which exploded on to the challenger's jaw. 'Man, he had me wobbling, I was hurt,' Bentt admitted. 'But I knew he could punch, that's why a big part of my training had to do with getting hurt – and how to react to it.

'There's two kinds of hurt in a ring when you get punched. One leaves you senseless and defenceless. But the other one is where your mind stays active, where you have the wherewithal to strike back. And that's how I was at that moment. Hurt but still thinking, still cunning. I knew that he knew I was in some trouble and I banked on him getting careless. I'd gone over that scenario a thousand times in my mind at training camp.'

The crowd roared, eagerly anticipating a spectacular and quickfire finish, as Morrison strode in to complete the demolition. But he was too confident, too casual, his hands were down as he moved forward. Bentt saw his chance – and he seized it, driving a mighty right-hander into the champion's unguarded jaw. Morrison crumbled to the canvas, his mouth open and his mind scrambled. He managed to claw himself up to beat the count, but he was now a man in dire distress, being pummelled unmercifully by a challenger who had suddenly become supercharged.

A fusillade of punches sent him tumbling again. Once more he climbed unsteadily to his feet. But his cause was now a hopeless one. Another barrage from Bentt sent him crashing for the third time. Under the WBO rules, that signalled the end of the fight. In just 93 sensational seconds, Michael Bentt, the man the world had written off, was a part champion of that world.

Sadly, the words he uttered in the sanctuary of his hotel room a couple of hours later were to prove prophetic. 'Remember that Andy Warhol line about everybody being famous for 15 minutes. Well, I guess that's me right now,' he said. His career, in fact, was to last only one more fight, when he lost his title to Herbie Hide in London five months later. Bentt, who had suffered fatigue problems training for that defence, performed lethargically before being knocked out in the seventh round. He was rushed to hospital after collapsing in his dressing-room and tests eventually showed a brain disorder which stopped him from fighting again.

His ambition now is to become a television boxing expert. I doubt, however, if he will ever witness a more spellbinding contest than his own greatest fight.

'They Can Never Take it Away from Me Now'

Frank Bruno v Oliver McCall

Frank Bruno was born in Hammersmith, London, on 16 November 1961. He first gained national prominence when he won the ABA heavyweight title while still a teenager in 1980. He never fought for the British title as a professional, but won the European title in 1985. He made four challenges for the world title, being stopped by Tim Witherspoon in 1986, Mike Tyson in 1989 and Lennox Lewis in 1993, before finally winning the WBC version by outpointing Oliver McCall at Wembley in 1995.

THE WHOLE WORLD wrote off Frank Bruno when he was pummelled to defeat by Lennox Lewis in the rain of Cardiff in October 1993. His enormous reserves of strength had kept him on his feet, but 15 unanswered punches from the WBC world heavyweight champion had left his brain concussed, his body quivering with pain and shock. It was surely the end of a career that had produced as many belly laughs as moments of belligerence. Bruno had become a national treasure, now he should be stored safely away from danger.

It was his third bruising defeat in his 11-year quest for the title. Tubby Tim Witherspoon had abruptly ended his first challenge, a well-below-par Mike Tyson had knocked him into oblivion the second time. Now Lewis, his fellow-Londoner, had left him a three-time loser. There was surely no way back for a man whose power had knocked over every journeyman and stool-pigeon placed in front of him, but patently lacked the speed, guile, stamina and defensive ability required at the top level. The pantomime stage was a far less demanding arena than the merciless ring.

Bruno, though, had different ideas. Within five months he was back in that ring, trampling over more cannon fodder. The same old Bruno, the same old story. But then two things conspired to give him a final chance he could never have dreamed of. Lewis, for once allowing his concentration to slip, was sensationally knocked out by Oliver McCall, an American of no previous punching prowess and a man who had spent much of his career as a sparring partner to the stars – Lewis, Bruno and Mike Tyson among them. McCall's promoter was Don King, who could barely believe that once again he had his hands on sport's richest prize, a title which eluded his grasp since the demise of Tyson. King had struck up a transatlantic alliance with British promoter Frank Warren. And when Bruno left Mickey Duff and Terry Lawless, the pair who had so skilfully guided him to fame and fortune, to join Warren's stable, he was promised a challenge at the eminently beatable McCall – and a fourth chance to finally grasp that cherished world title belt.

The politics of boxing being as morally dubious as they are, Bruno did not even have to defeat any worthy contender to cement that chance. While McCall struggled through a tedious defence against veteran Larry Holmes, Bruno was blasting aside a couple of ageing and abjectly cringing opponents in Shepton Mallett and Glasgow. That was enough to guarantee a 30,000 pro-Bruno audience at Wembley Stadium, so the date was set for 2 September 1995. Dear old Frank really did have the chance of a lifetime at last. And he knew it too. 'When he fought Holmes he looked amateurish. He was ordinary. I think I'm getting better as I get older. I'm wiser now. And I have the right team around me,' he said.

There was no question that his trainer George Francis had toughened him up, physically and mentally. Bruno had become a hard man in the ring, quite willing to use his elbows and his forearms, to rabbit-punch and to hold. And nobody could ever deny his desire. He locked himself away in a health farm in Leicestershire to hone an already fit body into an absolute peak. 'This is my business, this is my job – and this is my time,' he forecast, confidence and determination throbbing through his veins. He certainly bore the look of a man intent on achieving his destiny as he entered the ring grim-faced and utterly focused, ignoring the fireworks and the lasers which lit up the night sky.

McCall was a bundle of fretting agitation when he finally made his appearance, some 15 minutes later. There had been rumours that he had been involved in a heated row over his purse money and had even threatened to refuse to defend his title until he was persuaded to change his mind. Frankly, he seemed almost disinterested in proceedings in the early rounds, allowing Bruno to use his powerful left jab to build up a lead he was never to lose.

The champion finally began to fight back in the fifth round – 'I guess I was sleeping up to that juncture,' he admitted later – and as Bruno began to tire, his jab lost much of its early venom. To be truthful, the fight never matched the occasion, the action was often tedious. But the crowd roaring on their hero created their own dramatic intensity. This really was going to be Frank's big night – to hell with the quality, feel the excitement. And it did explode into almost unbearable tension in the late rounds when McCall, knowing that only a knockout or stoppage would nullify the sizeable lead Bruno had accumulated, launched a desperate assault.

In the last round in particular Bruno, his right eye reduced to a narrow slit by an ugly swelling, was battered almost without restraint as McCall summoned all the energy he had left for one furious last-gasp charge. Several times it seemed he was buckling – just as he had three times before. But, thankfully, McCall was no Lewis or Tyson, or even a Witherspoon. And Bruno had learned that the art of survival is as vital as any destructive qualities in the ring. He grabbed the champion round the waist, clutched him by his head, hugged him, did anything for temporary respite from the storm raging around him. Survive he did, to be mobbed by a ring-invasion army that included his stablemates Nigel Benn and Naseem Hamed.

When the unanimous verdict in his favour was announced, a taped rendition of Land of Hope and Glory blasted forth, more fireworks illuminated the vast stadium, the crowd roared their salute. They may not have been witness to an epic encounter, but they had watched one of British boxing's memorable occasions: Dear Old Frank had done it at last. An hour later, with dark glasses covering the scars of war, Bruno, in his own inimitable style, put his feelings graphically into words. 'I feel like ET turned inside out. My body's sore man, I got hit in the head and the bells were ringing. But I've dreamed of this moment for 14 years. I'm The Champ – and that's in the history books. If I get shot tomorrow, if I get run over by a bus, if I never walk again . . . they can never take it away from me now.'

It was impossible not to be moved by the eloquent simplicity of those words. No champion ever told it better. And some time later, when the euphoria had finally begun to abate, Bruno was also refreshingly honest about his achievement. 'I've never claimed I was a great fighter, I don't say now that I'm a great champion. I don't have the moves of someone like Muhammad Ali. But all I ever set out to prove was that by hard work and dedication you can achieve anything in this life. I hope I proved to all the kids out there that you don't have to go to university or have a brilliant brain to be successful. Just hard work and trust in the Big Man up there [rolling those great big eyes upwards] . . . that's what really counts.'

Bruno's reign was not to last very long. He was smashed to defeat by Tyson in Las Vegas in his first defence barely six months later. But his name remains there in the roll of honour of a title that has perhaps been cheapened on occasions by lesser champions than him since it was first fought for back in 1892. As he says: 'They can never take it away from me now.'

The Secret Superstar

Ken Buchanan v Ismael Laguna

Ken Buchanan was born in Edinburgh on 28 June 1945. He fought twice in the European Championships and won the ABA featherweight title in 1965 before turning professional later that year. A brilliant tactical boxer, he won the British lightweight title in 1968 and the world lightweight title two years later. He achieved a distinction no other European fighter has come close to equalling by topping the bill at New York's famed Madison Square Garden seven times.

IF ANY KNOWLEDGEABLE boxing supporter is asked to name his top half-dozen post-war British fighters, the name of Ken Buchanan is certain to be accorded a prominent appearance. The lean Scot from Edinburgh combined elegant skills with a razor-sharp tactical brain, a body as hard as his native country's granite and a total belief in his own destiny. He is probably the greatest lightweight these shores have spawned – and there are those who claim he is the greatest fighter, pound for pound, we have ever produced.

Yet Buchanan, in his halcyon days, was British boxing's best kept secret, a pugilistic prophet without honoured recognition in his own land. 'I could walk down any main street in Britain and be anonymous,' he says. Yet in America he was a cult figure, a hero to such a degree that the American Boxing Writers Association ignored their own to select him as their Fighter of the Year for 1970. That was a staggering accolade from a country never renowned for going overboard on the prowess of any Limey wearing boxing gloves. It is all the more remarkable to realise that those behind him in the poll included Muhammad Ali and Joe Frazier.

He had more than earned the achievement, however, because he had to defy the furnace-like 120-degree heat of a Puerto Rican afternoon as well as overcome a world champion who had already established his own reputation as a true ring craftsman. Ismael Laguna was a showman too, a fighter who brought a sense of style and occasion with him. 'We'd even heard he'd been living it up in the nightclubs in the weeks leading up to the fight. The local writers told us he'd been seen out at 11 o'clock at night,' said Buchanan. 'But it was music to me if it was true. It meant he wasn't taking my challenge too seriously.' Indeed, the backers of Laguna, the undisputed world lightweight champion, had instructed his American agent, Dewey Fregatta, to find him a 'soft' opponent as a warm-up for a massive pay-day that was looming against a rugged, up-and-coming challenger called Roberto Duran.

'They looked at my record and saw I had been beaten when I fought for the European title by a Spaniard called Miguel Velasquez. So they figured I must be a soft touch,' said Buchanan. 'What they didn't know was that I had clearly won the fight, only to be robbed by a home-town decision – the fight was in Madrid. I'd also not become a big name in Britain, even though I was the British champion by then.' Buchanan's problem was that he had engaged Welshman Eddie Thomas as his manager. Thomas was the guiding force behind the brilliant Howard Winstone, but he had fallen out with Harry Levene and Mickey Duff, who had a virtual monopoly on the major shows. So Buchanan was forced to spend most of his career to that point away from the big arenas and the national exposure of television. Indeed, most of his fights took place before the silent, dinner-suited audiences of sporting clubs, where applause was permitted only in the intervals between rounds. 'That's why Laguna and his camp thought they had nothing to fear,' he said. 'But I never doubted my own ability. I knew I had the skill and the experience to become world champion. It was only a question of getting the chance.'

Mind, when he stepped out of the aeroplane and on to the tarmac at San Juan, the heat overwhelmed him. 'If there had been a plane going straight back home, I'd have got on it,' he said. 'The heat was unbearable. It hit you as hard as any punch. It was suffocating. I had two weeks to try to get as used to it as I could before I went into the ring. But that was hopeless. You'd need two months to get anywhere near acclimatised. I'd been to places like

Spain on holiday before – and that got pretty hot. But this was ridiculous. I had to get up before five o'clock in the morning to do my running, before the morning sun came out.'

The contest had been arranged for Saturday, 26 September 1970 – at two o'clock in the afternoon, the hottest time of the day. 'I knew that just surviving 15 rounds in that pressure cooker would be an ordeal in itself,' said Buchanan. 'Initially, I had planned to fight a defensive, counter-punching performance, hoping that Laguna would wear himself out by chasing after me. But then we heard about his living it up – and also that he was having problems making the weight. That meant he would be likely to feel the effects of a fast pace in that heat even more than I would. So Eddie and I decided to change tactics. I would pressurise him, make him fight three minutes every round. That was the way to wear him down.'

Buchanan executed the tactics perfectly. From the first bell he moved in close to the champion, throwing punches constantly, never giving Laguna any time to compose himself or to take a respite from the furious pace. 'The heat was savage by the time we started. I heard later it was 120 degrees in the ring and the sun was beating down. It was merciless,' he said. 'My feet were starting to hurt me already by the end of the first round and the sweat was just pouring off me. It was like fighting in a sauna.' But Buchanan gritted his teeth and carried on grinding down his opponent. If he needed an extra motivation he had only to look at the champion's face. 'He was looking close to exhaustion as the rounds went by. That was a real comfort to me,' he said.

There were no knockdowns in the contest, which the Scot had dominated by his gameness as much as his genius. But when the final bell sounded, there was still a lingering doubt inside him. 'While the judges' scorecards were being counted up, my mind went back to that fight in Spain. I knew I had won that one, but the judges robbed me. I suddenly feared it could all go wrong for me again,' he said. 'Eddie Thomas and the rest of my corner were celebrating, but I just wanted it to be official first.' Then the announcement came . . . a split decision! 'That made it even worse,' said Buchanan. But thankfully, two of the judges had voted for him. 'I always knew I had the ability to become a world champion, but I was so knackered it was back in my dressing-room before it really sunk in,' he said.

It was a joyous party which returned to Britain – only to be shattered by the news that the British Boxing Board refused to recognise him as world champion. The WBC, the only world governing body of note at that time, had refused to sanction the contest and had stripped Laguna. And Britain's own rulers had backed them. 'It just about summed up the raw deal I always felt I got in my own country, as if powerful influences in the sport here just didn't want me to succeed,' said Buchanan. But over on the other side of the Atlantic, they were ready to salute him. And Buchanan returned as a hero, outclassing Californian/Mexican Ruben Navarro – the man the WBC had by now recognised as the champion – in Los Angeles to win universal recognition as the true king. Even the British Board recognised him after that.

He reigned as champion for two years, before the aforementioned Duran plundered his title when the Scot could not come out for the fourteenth round. That was hardly surprising. He had been the victim of a sadistic performance by the Panamanian wild man, who struck him with so many illegal blows – and even kneed him in the groin – that Buchanan could barely limp, let alone walk. But that defeat did not dent his immense popularity with the Americans. In all, he topped the bill at the famed Madison Square Garden in New York no fewer than seven times. 'I'm very proud of that – no European has done it before or since,' he says. 'And, after all, to be a success in another country is probably more of an achievement than being a winner in your own . . .'

Maybe the final accolade should come from the redoubtable Duran, one of the legends of boxing folklore. 'That man Buchanan – he was the hardest I ever faced, a true warrior,' he said. 'He ask me for a rematch and I tell him "No fear!". I tell him I never go near him again . . . and I never did.'

Simply the Best is Simply Bemused

Steve Collins v Chris Eubank

Steve Collins was born in Dublin on 21 July 1964. He moved to America to launch his professional career, basing himself in Boston where he quickly became a favourite among the large Irish community. After losing a points decision to WBA world middleweight champion Mike McCallum in 1990, he returned to Ireland to continue his career. He lost a split points decision to American Reggie Johnson for the vacant WBA title in 1992, but finally realised his dream of becoming Dublin's first world champion by stopping Chris Pyatt inside five rounds to win the WBO middleweight title two years later. He became a double world champion in 1995, stepping up to take the WBO super middleweight title from Chris Eubank – and inflicting on Eubank his first defeat.

CHRIS EUBANK always considered himself as boxing's Mr Cool. Whatever the drama of the occasion, whatever the provocation, he never let that mask of composure slip; his voice was never raised, even in the wildly hyped build-up to fights against bitter rivals Nigel Benn and Michael Watson. He always seemed the man in control. And that posturing self-confidence, allied to the grand manner of his spectacular entrances into the ring, had unnerved and overawed many an opponent. It had certainly played a sizeable part in the remarkable success of Eubank, who had remained unbeaten in 43 fights – 19 of them for world titles – and revelled in the glory of the Tina Turner song which became his ring anthem, 'Simply the Best'. 'Until I am beaten, I am The Man,' he would boast. It was difficult to argue. The quality of the opposition was occasionally dubious, but the showmanship he brought with him made him Britain's top sporting attraction. Television audiences of up to 14 million would watch: half the nation amused and captivated by his eccentricities, the other half simply desperate to see him dumped on his backside.

When Irishman Steve Collins took up the cudgels on 18 March 1995, it seemed to many like just another routine defence for the champion from Brighton. Collins was a rugged, tough campaigner who had come to England to stop Chris Pyatt inside five rounds in his last fight, to win the WBO world middleweight crown. But Pyatt's best days had gone. And so, many believed, had Collins's. He was 30 years old, two years older than Eubank, and was stepping up eight pounds to challenge for the WBO world super middleweight title.

But Collins was a fighter of a much greater pedigree than was generally appreciated this side of the Atlantic. He left his home in Dublin when he was 21 to pursue his professional career in America. He settled in Boston, America's most Irish city, and built up a powerful reputation. He took Mike McCallum, at the time a ferocious WBA world middleweight champion, the full 12 rounds and, despite losing, was driving the Jamaican backwards at the end. Then, when McCallum relinquished the title, he lost a split decision to Reggie Johnson, a clever and vastly underrated craftsman. Collins had not looked particularly impressive since his return to Ireland, until his comprehensive beating of Pyatt. 'The thing was that I needed a challenge to motivate me, to get me at full throttle,' he said. 'Pyatt was that challenge to a degree – it gave me the opportunity to become the first world champion ever to come from Dublin.

'But Eubank – that was something totally different. He was the most talked-about fighter of the day. Love him or hate him, nobody ever ignored him. Beating him would make me a millionaire – and, like all pros, I'm in this game for the financial security as well as the glory. I'd watched him a lot on television and I'd been at ringside a few times for his fights. And I knew enough about him to know that his tactics, the big entrances and the rest, used to intimidate opponents. He used to psyche them out. So I thought about the best tactics for me to use to turn the tables on him, to disturb his mind, get him worried and anxious.' In the end, the plan put into operation by Collins was simple and to the point: 'I decided to make him believe I was half-crazy, that he was fighting a madman!'

The plot was launched when the two were brought together in Dublin to publicise the contest, which was to be staged across the other side of Ireland, at the Green Glens Arena in Millstreet, a tiny hamlet in County Cork which was put on the map a couple of years previously when the Eurovision Song Contest was staged there. Collins accused the nattily attired Eubank of 'forgetting your African roots'. The champion was so infuriated he stormed away from Ireland and refused to go back until the weigh-in, the night before the contest. 'I thought Collins was a reasonably balanced man, but now he is a nonentity,' rapped Eubank. 'If I had my way I wouldn't talk to him, be in the same place – or even in the same country.' The outburst was music to Collins's ears. The first step of his unlikely, audacious mission had been accomplished . . .

Collins then took himself 6,000 miles away to Las Vegas to mount his intensive six-week preparation. The world's gambling capital seemed an odd choice – but there were no temptations to lure Collins from his goal. 'I never left my hotel room apart from my early morning run and my training in the afternoons,' he said. For recreation he used to sit and listen to the tapes made for him by his Irish friend and part-time sports psychologist Tony Quinn. 'It's a fast-growing area in sport. Even Mike Tyson used to see a psychologist in New York regularly. Boxing's a mental game as much as a physical one. And these people can help no end by boosting your confidence, teaching you how to relax, how to stay calm and in control of your nerves,' he said. 'I've seen so many fighters who look world-beaters in the gym. But they fall apart when they get in a ring, in front of a crowd. Why? Physically there's nothing wrong with them. If they had someone to help them mentally, they would be different altogether.'

But Collins decided to take the whole matter a lot further. The two fighters were paraded into the ring on the evening before the contest for their official weigh-in. This was 17 March, St Patrick's Night – and Eubank must have felt he was being attacked by leprechauns as Collins pursued him round the ring, constantly jabbing his fingers into the champion's chest and shouting at him, 'I'm gonna win, I'm gonna win . . .' Eubank was plainly startled by the antics, which provoked frenzied cheering from an astonishing audience of nearly 3,000 who had arrived to watch the preliminaries – such was the fanatical interest the fight had aroused. As Eubank eventually retreated to the sanctuary of the changing-room, Collins then let the word out that he was in a condition of deep hypnosis which would make him invincible when they fought. 'When I see Eubank's punches, they will be coming at me in slow motion!' he declared.

When Eubank heard – as Collins hoped he would – he was outraged. 'I cannot fight this man. It won't be Collins – it will be a man under a spell,' he said. 'Such things are dangerous and have no place in boxing. He could be killed or seriously hurt.' For two hours, while he should have been resting his mind and body, Eubank was in furious debate with promoter Barry Hearn. At first he was adamant that the fight was off. Only the persistence of Hearn persuaded the champion to change his mind. But there was one more surprise in store for him before the first bell would ring the next night . . .

Even by his own outrageous standards, Eubank's entry was spectacular. It seemed that half of Ireland had managed to find their way into the jam-packed arena and they gasped as the whole place plunged into darkness and then a spotlight showed the champion high above them, astride a Harley Davison motor-cycle which he revved furiously to add even more dramatic impact. As he was slowly lowered to the floor and the strains of Tina Turner accompanied him to ringside, even the partisan crowd roared their appreciation. But one man in the midst of the delirium was totally unmoved.

Collins, as the challenger, had made his entrance first. And while the Eubank carnival was in full flow, he had sat on his corner stool, the hood of his dressing gown pulled over his face – and a personal stereo wrapped round his ears, playing Irish music to drown out the champion's grand entrance. 'So many of his opponents have made the mistake of watching him, being spellbound, even frightened by it all. I knew I would have been trembling if I'd been watching,' he said. When Eubank eventually leapt over the top rope and into the ring, he looked across at an opponent who seemed to be fast asleep!

But Collins was certainly wide awake by the time the fight started. 'And I could sense, right from the off, that my tactics had worked on him. There seemed to be that little moment of hesitancy about everything he did,' said Collins. 'I knew he was a man who liked to fight at his own leisurely pace anyway. The way to defeat him was to keep the pressure on him constantly, never give him a moment to settle.' So the challenger swarmed over Eubank, hustling, bustling and sometimes brawling. It became a fascinating contrast of styles, with the champion attempting to assert a measure of control but rarely finding the time or the space to trap him. It must have felt, for Eubank, like fighting an eel that would constantly wriggle away from danger – and sting him for his pains.

If most of the quality punches were landed by Eubank, the sheer volume of the attacking frenzy launched against him had tilted the balance Collins's way by the time they came out for the seventh round. And then Collins brought pandemonium to an already wild-eyed crowd as he sent Eubank toppling with a sharp right hand to the champion's body. 'I knew it was a good shot – you can tell when they land right. So, when he got up, I went all out to finish him off. But give him credit, he was as strong as a bull,' said Collins.

Eubank was also brave enough to launch a desperate late rally to retain his title. In the tenth round, as Collins wilted under one frenzied attack, he was floored by a perfect right hook. 'It was a great shot – right on the button,' admitted Collins. 'But I was too close to that title now to let it slip from me. I was hurt, sure, but I was still feeling good, I still had enough strength left in me. I also knew that he would see this as his big chance. So I just looked up at him from the floor – and smiled. Then I waved my hand at my corner, to let them know that I was all right. That must have really made him mad, because when I got up he charged across the ring at me and threw this wild right hand. I just ducked and it sailed past me. He careered past me as well – and he finished up looking a bit silly.'

It was the last despairing fling for Eubank. At the end of 12 tumultuous rounds, Collins was declared the winner on a split decision. 'It was a moment I can never forget, the end of an absolutely perfect night and a perfect fight,' said the new champion. Not quite the end. The night dragged on until dawn as thousands of delirious Irishmen joined Collins and his team in celebration at his hotel in Killarney. But those pre-fight antics had caused consternation in boxing circles and the WBO asked for a rematch – a request to which Collins readily agreed. In Cork four months later there was no mention of hypnotism, no crafty strokes pulled. This time Collins relied solely on an incredible display of high-speed fury to leave Eubank flat-footed and open-mouthed in astonishment. All three judges voted for the Irishman. The legend of Chris Eubank, bruised and battered on that momentous night in Millstreet, was finally broken.

Bruises and Bubbly

John Conteh v Jorge Ahumada

John Conteh was born in Toxteth, Liverpool, on 27 May 1951. In a brilliant amateur career he won ABA national titles in 1970 and 1971, also capturing the gold medal at middleweight in the 1970 Commonwealth Games in Edinburgh. After turning professional he won the British, Commonwealth and European light heavyweight titles before outpointing Jorge Ahumada to become WBC world champion in 1974. Conteh has now become a popular after-dinner speaker.

YOU COULD LABEL John Conteh's career as the days of wine and bruised noses. Whenever and wherever he fought the champagne would always flow, and never more so than on the night of 1 October 1974, when he outpointed the durable Jorge Ahumada to capture the WBC world light heavyweight title. London town belonged to the 23-year-old kid from Liverpool in a celebration that started at the Playboy Club, one of his favourite haunts.

His manager and trainer, George Francis, eventually dragged him away to a Turkish baths in Jermyn Street, to let him sweat out the bruises and the soreness in his body – the testimony of a gruelling 15-round fight. But even there his fame and notoriety could not be hidden. 'Johnny Gold, boss of the Tramps nightclub across the road, heard where I was. So he came over with a big bottle of champagne in an ice-bucket for me!' grins Conteh. 'It was perfect. We drank the champagne and used the ice to ease the swellings on my face.'

It was a classic Conteh scenario: the handsome, hard-drinking, hell-raising heart-throb whose combination of skills and savagery inside the ring made him an irresistible figure for the fight fans and the smart set. He was as much at home in the West End night spots or at the wheel of a Rolls-Royce as in any sweaty gymnasium. He was the kid who struck gold that night, who had the whole world at his feet.

'This was the stuff of dreams for me at that stage of my life,' he admits. 'I never even wanted to box when I was a kid. I wanted to sing, to be in a band, but I didn't have anything like a good enough voice and I couldn't play an instrument. So boxing was the only way to make the money I needed to live that wild life. When you've known poverty in your childhood, I guess you set out wanting it all. That's why it's the poor who produce all the greatest boxers. It's their way to a richer and, you hope, a better life.'

Conteh's career had already been meteoric before he faced Ahumada. His dynamic ability and seemingly limitless potential had shown itself in his amateur days when he fought his way to two successive ABA titles at middleweight and then light heavyweight in 1970 and 1971. He had also brought home a middleweight gold medal from the 1970 Commonwealth Games in Edinburgh. He turned professional in 1971 and within little more than two years had already plundered the British, European and Commonwealth titles.

But he had so far faced nobody with the strength and the rugged durability of Ahumada, who had stunned the boxing world only four months previously by holding the 'invincible' champion Bob Foster to a draw. And he went to Foster's home town, Albuquerque, New Mexico, to do it. Foster, the 6ft 2in beanpole, stood head and shoulders over all challengers for eight years, but such was the shock of that fight that he immediately announced his retirement.

'I was there to see the fight, because I was hoping to get a crack at Foster,' recalled Conteh. 'In my mind, like in the opinion of a lot of good ringside observers, Ahumada won the fight. I was a bit disappointed that Foster didn't win because he was a legend – and I wanted to be the man to end his career. But when the fight with Ahumada was eventually made, for the vacant title, I knew how difficult an opponent he was going to be.'

The contest proved every bit as draining and exhausting as Conteh had anticipated. 'I had trained even harder than I ever had before this time. The only way I was going to outlast him was to be absolutely 100 per cent prepared. I sat in the dressing-room beforehand and went over every single facet of my training. Had I cheated on my roadwork one morning, had I maybe not put everything into one training session, did I cut any corners, miss the odd round of sparring? In every case the answer was no. So I knew that physically I was in my prime.

'Then I started to build myself up mentally, to get hatred for him inside me. Maybe not hatred, more a case of resentment. This man wanted to beat me up physically and to humiliate me. That made me fearful. And I used that fear to psyche myself up. I wouldn't let him; he was only human; he could be no fitter or stronger than me. And I knew I had more skill than him. And that's how I won the fight. He was every bit as strong as I had expected. He never gave an inch. But I had the edge in the way I could manoeuvre myself; I was that little sharper and quicker than he was.'

While there were no knockdowns, that was in itself a tribute to the strength and determination of the two protagonists, because the physical punishment suffered by them both was severe as neither man would wilt. For round after round they continued their unrelenting battle, seemingly ignoring the pain, unwilling to display any sign of distress. 'It's a mental thing,' says Conteh. 'Oh, I was hurting all right, same as I'm sure he must have been. But you don't show it, you don't show any sign of weakness. That can raise your opponent's morale, give him another ten per cent.'

Like all world title fights in those days, the contest was made over 15 rounds. 'Those last few rounds really were a case of mind over matter,' admits Conteh. 'Physically, I'd just about gone by that stage. It was a question of fighting by memory, letting your spirit drag you through.' The spirit of Conteh remained unbroken as he defied Ahumada's despairing late charge to win by 147 points to 142 on the scorecard of referee Harry Gibbs, who was also the sole judge. That gave him the vacant title by eight rounds to three, with four drawn.

Conteh was king, already amply justifying his illustrious rating as one of Britain's greatest post-war fighters. He was to retain the crown for nearly four years. But the champagne trail became increasingly dogged by splits within his camp. By the time he lost his title he had split with his manager and been involved in acrimonious legal action with his promoters. 'I felt I was worth more money,' he said. 'Looking back on it all now, I guess I made mistakes. But who doesn't in this business? Boxing's what I call an undisciplined discipline. You're taught all that aggression in the ring but while some fighters use it all up there, with others it spills over into their private lives. I guess that's what happened to me.'

The Punch that Shook the World

Henry Cooper v Cassius Clay

Henry Cooper was born in Westminster, London, on 3 May 1934. In a professional career stretching 17 years, from 1954 to 1971, he reigned for more than a decade as Europe's top heavyweight, holding the British, European and Commonwealth titles throughout most of the 1960s. He also challenged for the world title, but was stopped in the sixth round by Muhammad Ali. Cooper's modest demeanour outside the ring has made him one of Britain's enduring sporting heroes.

IT WAS the most famous punch ever thrown in a British ring. And to this day, more than 30 years on, people still talk wistfully of 'Enery's 'Ammer, the left hand of Henry Cooper that once floored Cassius Clay – and threatened for a few heart-stopping seconds, to change the whole course of world heavyweight history. 'If the punch had landed 20, even 10 seconds earlier, who knows what might have happened?' says the man who delivered it. 'Still, you can't change history. And I mustn't grumble. I've dined out on it ever since!'

Cooper, a true Cockney – born in Westminster, raised in Bellingham – was already the nation's favourite sporting son when he stepped into the ring at Wembley Stadium on the night of 18 June 1963 to face the brash, big-talking Clay. And this night he had the whole country behind him as never before. 'To put it bluntly, people wanted me to knock his block off. He'd been in London more than a week, telling everybody he was the greatest and the prettiest in the world, he was making up nursery rhymes to say what he was going to do to me. He was getting right up everybody's nose. I didn't mind because I was on a percentage of the gate, so the more he ranted on I knew the more people would turn up!'

In the event more than 44,000 supporters – a figure that has dwarfed any outdoor attendance in this country since – defied the drizzling rain to cheer their hero on. And what a tumultuous reception they gave Cooper as he bobbed his way to the ring first. 'You get a certain amount of nerves before any big fight,' says Cooper who, as the reigning heavyweight champion of Britain and the Commonwealth at the time, had already been involved in eight title contests. 'But this time it was totally different. This was so much more than just a fight. I knew I had the whole country urging me on. Right the way through my training, whenever anybody saw me they'd say the same thing: "Button that so and so's big mouth!"

'I used to get up at quarter to four every morning to do my roadwork, running round the streets and past the gasworks. There was this old grandmother, an office cleaner, who used to be going to work at the same time. The old gal would give me a cheer every time I went past her. Then even she would say: "You do it for all of us, 'Enery, you go in there and knock him out, shut him up!" It's funny when you think how Clay, after he changed his name to Muhammad Ali, would become such a well-loved person over here. Even when he was hated by the whites in America, who called him a draft-dodger because he wouldn't go to Vietnam, the people here liked him. By then we could all see that all the nonsense he talked was really just tongue in cheek. But there's no question that in them days he wasn't the British people's cup of tea.'

If Cooper entered the ring at Wembley to a hero's welcome, I doubt if Hitler's arrival would have provoked much more rage than the swaggering entrance of Clay, who strode regally down the aisle and climbed through the ropes wearing a cardboard crown! 'That got the punters even more angry. But I just ignored him. If he wanted to look like a village idiot, that was up to him,' says Cooper. There was no doubting the impressive credentials of Clay who, at just 21 years old – eight years younger than Cooper – was already pressing for a challenge at the world heavyweight title. He had captured the gold medal at the 1960 Olympic Games in Rome when he was only 18 and had then embarked on a barnstorming, unbeaten professional career, telling the world of his genius, making predictions before most of his fights – and usually proving them right.

'I knew he was very mobile and quick-moving for a heavyweight. Although I was a bit quicker than average, I realised I couldn't beat him at long range. So the plan was to get the fight to close range whenever possible,' said Cooper. The strategy worked like a dream in the opening round as Cooper drew blood from Clay's nose with one sharp left hook and generally roughed him up. 'I could see already how nimble he was – he moved like a middleweight. But I was amazed how little he knew about fighting inside. He was a novice. I was able to give him a bit of a going-over. I caught him with a few good uppercuts. He just didn't know how to stop them – he didn't know how to fight what some people might call a dirty fight.'

Cooper had just as much success in the second round as the huge crowd roared him on, perhaps beginning to sense that a sensation was starting to unfold before them. But in round three, with only 40 seconds gone, Cooper emerged from one close-range encounter with blood spurting from a cut over his left eye. It was the crimson message his supporters most dreaded – the old jinx had struck again, at the most crucial moment of his fighting life. Cooper's career had been plagued by cuts around his eyes, where his skin tissue had always been susceptible to blows. 'But nobody ever cut me as bad as Clay did,' he says. 'At first I thought it was a butt, but it wasn't. He used to throw out them cutting punches, long, flicking jabs that used to twist as they landed. This time I think he caught me with the heel of his glove and that just opened up the cut.'

It certainly brought fresh enthusiasm to Clay, whose hands hung down alongside his hips as he began to taunt the stricken Cooper, clowning and even pulling faces at him. Cooper, pausing occasionally to wipe away the blood that was blocking his vision, tried to carry on, gamely taking the fight to the American. He did manage to survive the round, but his manager Jim Wicks wanted to end the fight as Henry sat on his stool. 'I knew how bad the cut was. But I was arguing with Jim, I wanted to give it another go, just one more round. He wouldn't have it, he was trying to call the referee Tommy Little over to stop it. So I got my gumshield in quick and jumped off the stool into the ring ready for the next round before he could stop me,' said Cooper.

Within seconds of round four beginning the cut was opened again. Clay, now the goading, braying predator, teased and tormented Cooper for the next two and a half minutes, flicking his jab into the wound with almost unerring accuracy, causing the blood to spill ever more freely. But Cooper, having to wipe away the blood constantly by this stage, still managed to ruffle his tormentor with a couple of good left hooks. Then, just three seconds from the end of the round, came the moment, the punch, that was to take its place in history. Clay was dancing in front of him, a sneer on his handsome face, when Cooper unleashed a thunderbolt of a left hook that landed flush on the American's jaw. Pandemonium erupted around the ringside as Clay went crashing. He sprawled on the bottom rope, his right hand stretched over the middle rope. Then he slowly sank to the canvas, the life seemingly drained from his face.

Cooper's left hook was his trademark, a punch that had already despatched many of his opponents. He knew the damage it could inflict. 'When you hit a guy, his eyes tell you everything,' he says. 'Joy, pain, anguish. When I looked down at him, he just had a blank look. I knew then it was a good shot I'd hit him with.' Such was Clay's semi-conscious state that he did not possess the inbuilt instinct of a badly hurt but still thinking fighter to allow the count to give him a few precious extra seconds to unscramble his mind. Instead, he hauled himself up, his face still devoid of expression, at the count of three, and staggered dazedly along the ropes to his own corner.

He was totally unaware that the bell had ended the round, giving him precious sanctuary – but Cooper was, to his unbridled frustration. 'He was out of it. If I could have had just a few more seconds to get to him again I could have finished him off. I also knew how bad my eye was. There wasn't much time left for me. But he was so badly hurt I didn't know if he could recover in the minute's break.' In the event, the interval lasted more than two minutes after Clay's glove was discovered to be split. 'In them days there was no second pair of gloves ready at the ringside for such an emergency,' said Cooper. 'They had to send someone to the dressing-room to get a new pair. By the time all that pantomime took place, the interval was twice as long as it should have been. It gave Clay the time he needed to pull himself together.'

It has been argued to this day that the damage to Clay's glove was caused, quite deliberately, by his own cornermen to give their man that vital breathing space. 'I don't know about that,' says Cooper. 'Angelo Dundee, who was Clay's trainer, always denied it to me. But maybe he saw a bit of a split in the glove and helped it on its way a little bit. At the time I didn't know what was going on. I was sat in my corner and my cornermen were covering my view of it all. But watching it on television later, I saw one of his men break a phial and hold what seemed to be ammonia under his nose to bring him round. That was blatantly illegal. But with all that was going on at the time I guess it was impossible for anyone to keep a grip on the situation.'

Ironically, it was this fight which persuaded the British Boxing Board of Control to change their rules, to ensure that two spare pairs of gloves were always kept at ringside in future, in case of any similar mishap. It came too late for poor Cooper, though. The long break had resuscitated Clay. And Dundee, as cute and sharp a cornerman as you could ever find, had also used the time to read the riot act to his fighter. 'No more clowning around, cut out the nonsense. Get out there and do a job of work before he hits you again,' he screamed at his boxer. Clay heeded the message to the letter. There was a look of grim determination on his face as round five belatedly began. It was to last little more than a minute for Cooper, whose cut was split open again so badly by the profusion of punches now coming from Clay that even Henry's own supporters were shouting for the bloodbath to be ended, before referee Little stepped in.

'I was so sick – because I didn't think he beat me because he was a better puncher or a better technician,' said Cooper. 'He beat me because I had this bloody weakness! I knew I was doing pretty well in the fight. If you'd counted up the cards when it was stopped, I would have been ahead.'

Clay went on to capture the world title eight months later, beating Sonny Liston. He came back to London again in 1966 to defend his crown – this time a real one! – against Cooper in 1966. It was a bloody replica of their first meeting, with Cooper stopped on cuts in the sixth round this time.

'He was a much smarter fighter by then, he knew how to fight on the inside, how to hold on, put you off balance, things like that,' recalls Cooper. 'We became good pals later. I got to genuinely like the guy. I think I earned his respect that night at Wembley, though. Maybe he had been belittling me before the fight, but he said something afterwards I'll never forget. He talked about the punch which put him down and admitted: "That Cooper hit me so hard, he didn't only shake me – he shook my relatives in Africa!"'

Every Dog Has its Day

Buster Douglas v Mike Tyson

James 'Buster' Douglas was born in Columbus, Ohio, on 7 July 1960. As a schoolboy his favourite sport was basketball, but he gave up a potential career on court to become a professional boxer when he was 20. He was stopped in the tenth round by Tony Tucker in his attempt to win the vacant IBF world heavyweight title in 1987, but scored the most unexpected victory in heavyweight history in Tokyo in 1990, when he knocked out Mike Tyson in the tenth round to become the undisputed world champion.

JAMES DOUGLAS was given his nickname Buster as a baby, 'because I used to cry all night long, just like a puppy dog. Buster meant Bad – what's why they called me that name. I guess it stuck with me ever since.' There were those who claimed that the 'dog' had remained inside him right into his adult fighting life. Such a term is highly derogatory in boxing: it suggests a fighter who lacks heart and courage, whose will and spirit can be broken. In truth, it was difficult to argue against the claim.

Douglas had much basic, natural talent but his desire had always been questionable. He seemed to simply surrender to Tony Tucker when they fought for the vacant IBF world heavyweight title in Las Vegas in 1987, dominating the contest and then crumbling when Tucker launched a desperate rally in the tenth round. Mike Tyson, who held the WBC and WBA titles, topped that bill, blasting veteran Pinklon Thomas to sixth-round defeat in his all-conquering march. Tyson was to add the IBF crown to his collection, outpointing Tucker three months later. As for Douglas . . . oblivion beckoned.

Maybe he wasn't all that bothered. After all, he had never really wanted to become a fighter. In his schooldays basketball was his passion. In the end, though, he bowed to the wishes of his father. Billy 'Dynamite' Douglas had been a decent boxer in the 1960s and 1970s. He never quite made it to the top, but the dream continued when his career ended – carried on by the oldest of his four sons. Billy Douglas became a small-hall promoter in the family home town, Columbus, Ohio, also finding the time to manage and train his boy through his early years as a professional.

But the father-son relationship – invariably a problem area in a sport of licensed brutality – ended with that defeat by Tucker. Douglas might have quit the ring altogether, had he not met John Johnson, a one-time football coach who became his manager. Johnson knew little about boxing, but he was a brilliant motivator. He instilled a fresh sense of belief and confidence into Douglas. Together they forged a relationship that was to stun the entire world less than three years later.

While Douglas was rebuilding his career with solid if unspectacular points victories over veteran Trevor Berbick and Oliver McCall, Mike Tyson's life was heading dangerously out of control. His marriage to Robin Givens had collapsed, he had got rid of the people who had been alongside him on his way to the undisputed title, the controversial Don King had taken over as his promoter and mentor – and amid the lurid rumours of his wayward lifestyle, his appetite for boxing had become open to question. He pulled out of a title defence against Canadian Razor Ruddock, a top contender and, in the view of many good judges, a highly dangerous opponent for a champion who might not be up to his former destructive standard. Instead, with Ruddock fuming, King and Tyson took off to Japan, where they agreed a multi-million-dollar title defence in Tokyo on 11 February 1990. They then looked around for what the fight trade calls 'a warm body', an opponent who would be grateful to collect a challenger's cheque for a million dollars and would be unlikely to present much opposition in the ring. Buster Douglas fitted the bill perfectly. Those wins over Berbick and McCall gave him some credibility, but they were yawning fights. Buster's lack of heart was matched by his lack of power.

The Japanese didn't mind, because Tyson was the only warrior they wanted to see. He had fought in the same arena, the colossal,

65,000-capacity Tokyo Dome, three years previously and thrilled a huge audience with a two-round knockout of Tony Tubbs. They wanted him back.

Douglas caused hardly a raised eyebrow as he arrived in Tokyo a month before the contest, on the same plane as Tyson. Not that the challenger noticed. His whole life was in turmoil back home. Douglas had been first involved in family tragedy three years earlier when one of his brothers was accidentally shot dead as a gun he was cleaning went off. Douglas had become a born-again Christian in July 1989, but that did not stop his wife leaving him two months later. Then he discovered that a former girlfriend, the mother of his 11-year-old son, was dying of cancer. But the most savage blow of all came just three weeks before the fight, while he was in Japan, when his mother Lula died. Douglas was heartbroken. But in the end, all that personal tragedy was turned into the pillars of his sensational triumph. Especially the death of his mother. He sobbed openly when the news was broken to him. He was to say later, with no flickering trace of exaggeration: 'I was prepared to die when I went in the ring with Tyson. What's the worst thing that can happen to you? The death of your mother, that's what. After that, it didn't matter to me much if I lived or died against Tyson.'

The world remained far more interested in the woeful pre-fight form of Tyson than the growing determination of Douglas. Pictures were flashed around the globe when Tyson was knocked down in training by a sparring partner, Greg Page. But still any talk of an incredible upset was laughed off. Back in America, such was the derision heaped upon Douglas that even in the casinos of Las Vegas, where you can lay odds on the first man on Mars or the next sighting of Elvis, there was no gambling interest in the fight. Only one casino even bothered to open a book. And they could find no takers for Douglas – even at odds of 42–1, the longest ever for a world title fight.

But two men across the other side of the Pacific Ocean didn't care. Douglas worked harder than he had ever done before in the weeks leading to his moment of destiny. It was his way of therapy for the cruel fortunes fate had handed him. And John Johnson's motivational skills were now in evidence – to supreme effect. 'You are looking unbeatable, you can knock out Tyson . . .' The message became a constant theme, blasted into his ears with unfailing regularity. Douglas responded. 'I had no fear in me, like a lot of Tyson's opponents had when they faced him. I had nothing, absolutely nothing left to lose,' he said later.

The contest took place at nine o'clock on Sunday morning, Tokyo time, to accommodate Saturday night television audiences back in America. The massive indoor arena was surprisingly only half full. Either the Japanese had also written off Douglas, or rising at that unearthly weekend hour was more of a sacrifice than they were prepared to make. But Buster was certainly wide awake. He was off his stool and bounding into the centre of the ring before the first bell. He stayed there, refusing to take a backward step as Tyson advanced, clipping the champion with his left jab and tying him up inside. There was no sign of intimidation here. And no foolhardy bravado either.

Tyson had made short, painful work of opponents who, hysterical with fear, had charged at him, arms flailing – and leaving their chins exposed for the champion to extract brutal retribution for their insubordination. But Douglas, at 6ft 3ins a good four inches taller and with a longer reach, was using those attributes wisely. 'A big man with mobility, a good jab – and with courage – will beat Tyson because he has the tools needed,' Angelo Dundee, once the mentor of Muhammad Ali, had told me long before this fight, when Tyson seemed unbeatable. Now that prophecy was coming true, as Douglas continued to dominate proceedings against a champion who was slow and sluggish – and becoming increasingly depressed.

As the rounds went by, Douglas grew in confidence. He was hitting Tyson with his jab almost at will, he was using his nimble movement to frustrate the champion's own attacks. And, far from being intimidated, he was quite prepared to use the dubious measures that had long been a feature of Tyson's own armoury. He punched the champion after the bell, smashed his elbow into Tyson's face, he even took a swipe at him when referee Octavio Meyran pulled them apart. By the fifth round Tyson's left eye had begun to swell ominously, testimony to the damage being inflicted by a challenger who now seemed to have established a total mastery.

It was an almost eerie scenario. The Japanese audience sat in almost total silence, breaking out into polite applause only at the end of each round. In America, the crowd would have raised the roof at the spectacle of Tyson, the self-professed 'baddest man on the planet', being pummelled and humbled by such a rank outsider. But, as both men began to tire, Tyson launched one big, despairing assault in the eighth round that came so close to undoing all the prodigious effort Douglas had given. The champion ducked underneath a jab and then threw a right uppercut that carried every ounce of his remaining strength and power. It was a ferocious punch that jolted Douglas's head so violently it seemed that his face had exploded as he toppled backwards on to the canvas. It was as devastating a punch as Tyson has ever thrown. Yet, astonishingly, Douglas was quickly back on his knees, his mind aware enough to be listening to the referee, counting over him. It seemed an eternal count – it was timed later at 13 seconds – but Douglas could only react to the numbers he heard from referee Meyran. He climbed to his feet at nine, with the bell ringing immediately to give him another precious minute to restore his mind and body.

He comfortably warded off Tyson's early attacks in round nine and came back with a vicious assault of his own to have the champion reeling against the ropes by the end. By that stage it was obvious that Tyson's desperate rally had been in vain. In round ten, Douglas produced his own lethal brand of execution with a cluster of punches which were to reverberate around the whole shocked world. A crunching right uppercut sent Tyson reeling backwards, then, before he could fall, a four-punch combination – two right hands and two lefts – rained in on him. Tyson's head hit the floor with such force that his gumshield fell out. He tried in vain to catch it, then scrambled on his hands and knees to look for it. He stuffed a part of it into his mouth and tried valiantly to climb to his feet. But his legs had no strength left. As he rose, he lurched drunkenly into the referee's chest, clutching him for support.

The result was declared a knockout, although technically it was a stoppage by the referee as Tyson was actually on his feet, unsteady and unanswering as they were, at the end. But that was a trivial argument. The fairytale reality, now being relayed to a stunned world, was that James 'Buster' Douglas, the no-hoper from Palukaville, was the new, undisputed heavyweight champion of that world. Mike Tyson, the unbeatable, the ring-monster, was vanquished. Or was he?

Douglas was in tears as he talked to a crowded press conference. 'I did it for my mother,' he said. Tyson was nowhere to be seen. He had locked himself away in his hotel suite. But Don King, once the disbelief at what he had witnessed had turned to recognition of grim reality, was busy. He was loudly claiming that Tyson should be declared the victor because he had knocked out Douglas first, harking back to the 13 seconds the challenger had been on the floor.

It was a ludicrous argument, because Douglas had merely acted on the count of the referee – just as Gene Tunney had in his infamous 'long count' victory over Jack Dempsey 64 years earlier. But at one stage it seemed as if Douglas's glory was to be snatched away from him as the presidents of both the WBC and the WBA sided with King and threatened to declare the title vacant. Thankfully, some kind of honesty prevailed eventually and 24 hours after his epic victory Douglas was officially recognised as champion. 'Now I just want to get into my boat and go fishin',' he said. A classic epitaph from the man who had just hooked himself a whale. The Man Who Beat Mike Tyson.

A Funny Thing Happened . . .

Mickey Duff v Kenny Green

Mickey Duff was born in Drohobitz, Poland, on 7 June 1929. His father, fearful of the growing threat to the Jewish people throughout central Europe, moved his family to Britain in 1938. They settled in East London where he grew up to become one of the most successful managers and promoters in the world.

MICKEY DUFF has been Mr Boxing to millions of the sport's followers throughout the world for the past 30 years. As a manager and promoter he has been involved with no fewer than 15 world champions and his face has become more famous than any of them. He has built up a vast knowledge of the fight game over the decades and is probably its leading authority on either side of the Atlantic. Yet what is not generally known is that Duff had a remarkable fighting career of his own before he turned his talents towards the safer side of the ring.

He had 123 amateur fights and fought 69 times as a professional – and still retired two months before his 20th birthday! 'I had my first amateur fight when I was 11½ years old. And I reckon I lost as many as I won,' he said. 'But I learned how to make money out of it. Every Saturday afternoon in those days there were amateur shows all over London. I'd look up where they were being held in the *Boxing News* and then I'd be off with my kit to the nearest one. If there wasn't a spot for me there, I'd move on to the next one until I got a fight.

'You always got a canteen of cutlery or the like for fighting – it was strictly amateur of course. But I'd take that and then go and flog it for ten bob! So I'd started getting some lessons about how to make a few quid even before I turned pro. That was when I was 15 years and four months old – the minimum age then was 16, but I lied about my age and nobody seemed to bother too much about checking it. I was just a tiny thing when I started, a bantamweight, although I finished up four years later as a welter – I must have been starting to eat better!

'Of my 69 pro fights I only lost eight and drew three – I won the rest. But I knew by the time I was 19 that I didn't have what it takes to make it to the top, to become a champion. That's why I quit. I only had such an impressive record because I used to manage my manager – I used to make sure the fights I had weren't too tough.'

Duff was managed by Alf Jacobs, a man from a well-known boxing family. 'We'd fight all over London. In those days there were shows every week at dozens of small halls and arenas all over town. I was fighting every two or three weeks, making a living and managing to win most of the time. But the fight I'll always remember, my greatest performance if you'd like to call it that, was in truth a fight I knew very little about!

'I was taking on this kid called Kenny Green at the Mile End Arena. He came from Croydon and he was a bit of a banger. It was about my 15th fight – I was just 17 years old. It was only a six-round fight and I remember starting pretty well for the first couple of rounds. Then – Bang! I was on the deck for the first – and the only – time in my career. How I got there I don't quite recall. I think it was a left hook.

'The strange thing is I didn't feel hurt, I just felt like I was floating in a dream. I don't even remember getting up. I just remember boxing my way out of any further trouble for the rest of that third round. I got back to my corner at the bell, pleased I had shown I could survive a knockdown. There were still three rounds to go and I was feeling well enough to get back to my boxing and beat this guy Green by being a bit more skilful. So imagine my surprise when the timekeeper suddenly called "Sixth and last round" as he sounded the bell. I'd fought through two rounds while still being concussed by that punch which put me down. What happened to rounds four and five is something I'll never know until my dying day.

'I was told by people at the ringside later that I had won both rounds – in fact, according to the referee I had won every round of the six bar the third. And apparently, so people said, I'd fought like a lunatic, throwing my natural caution to the wind. I must have been knocked senseless! But it certainly taught me to be a whole lot more careful in the rest of my fights.'

While Duff learned at an extraordinarily early age that there was to be no great pot of gold waiting in the ring for him, he had already fallen in love with the sport that was to dominate his life. Within eight months of retiring he had gained a match-maker's licence and his new career blossomed from there. Perhaps he had his toughest fight of all in his early days as a promoter when he once had to eject a couple of rough-looking customers from front row seats they had not paid for. Ronald and Reggie Kray were far from happy at the treatment! But it helped to build Duff's reputation as a man who would take such arrogant behaviour from nobody.

He does not believe that his own boxer's background has been of any help in his years on the other side of the ring. 'Maybe it did give me a bit of insight into the mind of a fighter, but really the two things are different as chalk and cheese,' he says. 'Boxers are paid to fight. The harder they train, the more they are dedicated, the more successful they will become and the more money they will make.

'But a manager has to be a psychiatrist, he has to get his fighter mentally right, he has to organise his training schedules, make sure he gets the right kind of opposition, he has to be a good judge of talent, to spot potential in a 16-year-old kid. He has to have an accountant's brain, he has to be thick-skinned to criticism. And he has to be durable. Running round the world arranging fights can be as knackering as actually fighting!'

The Glory of a Mug's Game

Chris Eubank v Nigel Benn

Chris Eubank was born in Dulwich, London, on 8 August 1966. He begin his professional career in the USA in 1985, winning five contests before returning to England. He captured the WBO world middleweight title from Nigel Benn in 1990, defending it three times before moving up to win the WBO super middleweight title the following year. He successfully defended that title a remarkable 14 times in three years before finally losing the title – and his unbeaten record – to Ireland's Steve Collins in his 44th contest in 1995.

'WHO'S FOOLING WHO?' was the question screaming out across the top of the fight posters advertising Nigel Benn's defence of his WBO world middleweight title against Chris Eubank. It was a valid inquiry – more than that, it was the $64,000 question – as far as the challenger was concerned. Back in the autumn of 1990, Eubank had already established himself as the most outspoken and controversial British boxer of his time. But could he fight? He was still unbeaten after 24 contests, but that had been very much the learning part of his career, against opponents who were highly unlikely to blemish that record.

Now he was stepping up dramatically to face the most ferocious fighting machine of the day – and a champion who self-admittedly hated him. 'He's the only guy in boxing I've ever actively disliked. I can't stomach him because of the way he puts down boxing,' said Benn. Like so many of his fellow professionals, Benn had been enraged by Eubank's oft-repeated claim that 'boxing is barbaric. It's a mug's game. I'm only in it for the money. As soon as I have what I need I will be off – and you will never see me in the ring again.' The animosity between them, on Benn's part especially, reached such a level of intensity that it threatened to boil over into violence several times at press conferences before their scheduled encounter at Birmingham's vast National Exhibition Centre on 18 November.

The vast majority of the country sided with Benn. He was the warrior king, the champion who travelled to America to win his title after his early career was rudely gatecrashed by Michael Watson, who stood up to a five-round onslaught and then clinically knocked him out in the sixth. Benn had shown the character and the courage to recover from adversity. He had come back to England as a hero and the swashbuckling bravado he carried into the ring with him always made for edge-of-the-seat excitement and drama. Eubank, by contrast, was a much more measured, cautious performer. His stand against the sport which paid his wages had already marked him as a contentious and somewhat eccentric character – the kind the British love to hate.

'I have never regretted what I said. To my mind I was only standing up for other boxers – including Nigel Benn,' says Eubank. 'A lot of fighters are exploited by managers and promoters. They are manipulated. They are the ones who take the pain and the punishment. They should have more control over their destiny.'

As for Benn, he insists: 'I never hated Nigel. I never set out to needle him. All boxers are brave men, warriors. I don't hate any of them. I admire them.'

But that did not prevent a totally tunnel-visioned approach to the contest from the challenger. After the acrimony of their earlier press conferences, Eubank refused to share the dais with Benn in the week leading to the fight. Instead he locked himself away from the world. Even after he arrived in Birmingham he remained in his hotel room in the vast NEC complex, away from public glare. He stayed there until a couple of hours before the fight was due to begin. Then he went for a walk, accompanied by his trainer Ronnie Davies and another close friend, Andy Ayling, who was at the time a press officer for his promoter Barry Hearn.

He pulled the collar of his coat over his face and put on a pair of sunglasses to avoid being recognised by the thousands of fans jostling to enter the arena. Then the three walked to a deserted carpark, where Eubank engaged in a few minutes' shadow boxing to warm himself up, then aimed one final punch into the chilled night air before proclaiming: 'I'm ready. Let's do it.' 'I don't recall another word being spoken. We just walked quietly back to his room, where we collected his gear,' said Ayling. 'No words were needed. He had no doubts within himself that he was going to win. I've never known any man so totally focused.'

Eubank was indeed a man utterly determined not to be upset by any obstacle. As the challenger he had to make the first entry into the ring, jeered by a capacity crowd who, almost to a man, were rooting for Benn. That did not bring a trace of emotion to his face. Even when the booming accompanying music of Tina Turner's 'Simply the Best' was suddenly strangled while in full flow – his team claimed sabotage by someone in Benn's camp – Eubank refused to be ruffled. 'Accept it – no moaning,' he told them. This was his night of destiny. And nothing or nobody was going to deny him.

Benn, as he had threatened, stormed to the attack from the start. His plan was to overwhelm a challenger who had never fought in such a highly charged atmosphere before, who might suffer from stage-fright. But if the champion was cast in the role of the irresistible force, Eubank was the quite immovable object. He refused to take a backward step, instead he met the challenge head-on. So from the outset it became a brutal bar-room brawl of a contest: two men too proud to give way, both driven by the same primitive instinct to inflict savage punishment. For round after bludgeoning round the warfare continued, if anything intensifying as the night wore on.

By the end of the sixth round, the halfway mark, there was nobody present who still questioned Eubank's heart or his desire. While the soreness which already gripped his body was testimony to the power of Benn, the champion was in even greater distress. A vicious swelling had begun to form under Benn's left eye from the early rounds. By now it had swollen so much that the eye was little more than a narrow slit above it. Benn could barely see from that left eye. It was a vivid, ugly confirmation of Eubank's own punching power – and his accuracy. His punches had carried more cruel authority than Benn's. The challenger was on his way to the title.

But not for nothing was Benn venerated as a supreme warrior. From those depths of desperation, with only one eye to give him vision, he launched himself into a mighty assault. In the eighth round a swinging overarm right, catching Eubank off balance, sent him tumbling to his knees. It was the first time, for all the naked aggression, that either man had been off his feet. The crowd were in uproar as they sensed the kill.

Eubank hauled himself to his feet and managed to weather the storm. And with that went Benn's final fleeting chance to turn the fight around. A left hook sent the exhausted champion reeling on to the ropes in round nine. Half a dozen punches rained in on him as he leant there, quite unable to summon the energy to pull himself clear. The final punch was a big overhand right – Eubank's most blistering weapon – which left Benn in such distress he was about to keel over until American referee Richard Steele rushed in to stop the slaughter and hug the beaten champion, to prevent him from the indignity of falling. It was over; Eubank was the new champion. Referee Steele captured the whole gripping drama when he declared: 'That was the toughest fight I was ever involved in. How they took the punishment I'll never know. Those two guys are both heroes.'

Eubank had finally allowed his own mask to slip in the high emotion of his victory. In the middle of his television interview, while still in the ring, he suddenly broke off to send a personal message to his girlfriend Karron – mother of their baby son Christopher – who was watching from their home in Brighton. 'Marry me now, Karron, please marry me,' he yelled tearfully into the microphone. The couple were wed a few months later. But for now, once he had finally retreated to his hotel room, all Eubank could feel was pain – in every bruised and battered inch of his face and body. 'It was pain like I'd never known before,' he said. 'That's why I said "never again" when someone suggested a rematch with Benn. I never wanted to see that man opposite me in a ring again in my life.'

The new champion even needed stitches to a painful cut on his tongue, caused when Benn punched him in the mouth while he was lifting his gumshield with his tongue to enable him to gulp in air. There were no celebratory noises from either Eubank or the team members in his room. He was in too much distress for that. 'I can't even raise my arms,' he told them. So they had to help him into the shower, then wash him down. That's when the first moment of humour broke through. 'We washed him all over, every inch of his body bar one part, which you can guess. Nobody would do that. In the end Ronnie Davies brought a saucepan full of water, put it in front of him and told him he had to wash that part of his body himself! That finally had everybody laughing,' said Ayling.

Eubank did not surface until the next morning when, by chance, he came face to face with Benn in the hotel foyer. The two hugged each other. There was no animosity between them at this moment, only the total respect each had earned from the other on that unforgettable night before.

The Hod Carrier Lifts Gold

Chris Finnegan v Alexi Kiselev

Chris Finnegan was born at Cawley, near Uxbridge, Middlesex, on 5 June 1944. He won a gold medal in the middleweight division in the 1968 Olympic Games in Mexico before turning professional. He lost a challenge for the European middleweight title before moving up to light heavyweight, where he became British, Commonwealth and European champion. But he was knocked out by American Bob Foster in his only world title contest.

CHRIS FINNEGAN declares, with the uncompromising bluntness that characterised his fighting career, 'When you've been an 'od carrier, carting round half a hundredweight of bricks on your back eight hours a day, boxing was easy.' It was never that for the second of the three Finnegan brothers – his older brother Terry was once an Irish champion and Kevin, the youngest of the three, became British and European middleweight king. Chris also plundered the British and European crowns, as a light heavyweight, in his professional career – and he added the Commonwealth title to his list for good measure. He did not quite make it to the very summit as a pro, being knocked out in the 14th round of an epic challenge to the powerful American world champion Bob Foster in 1972. In those days Finnegan was a man who fought with his heart on his sleeve. Every contest was a brutal and generally bloody exhibition of trench warfare. Yet in his earlier amateur years, Finnegan was renowned more for his skills and ringcraft than for the tearaway style he was later to adopt.

Steve Collins welcomes Chris Eubank to Ireland . . .
and then invites him to take a seat!

The Little and Large Show . . . Lennox
Lewis with his manager Frank Maloney
(left) and Frank Bruno with his former
manager Mickey Duff

Now it's time for business for Lewis (left) and Bruno

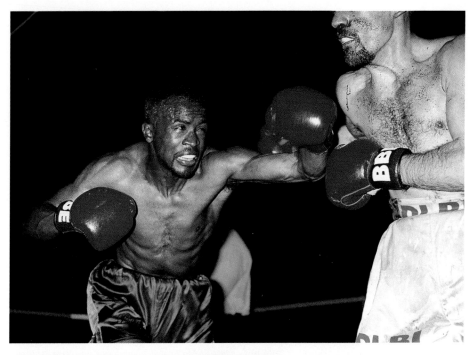

Colin McMillan powers his way to world title glory

. . . But his pal Duke McKenzie enjoys a double celebration

Champions at the mike . . . Sky's ringside expert Glenn McCrory (above) and Jim Watt with his wife

The thrill of victory . . . Steve Robinson (left) and Evander Holyfield celebrate

The mean machines . . . Chris Eubank and Nigel Benn admire Eubank's Harley Davison

The mean machine . . . Ed Robinson is ready to rumble

*Even Heavies can be friendly . . . Mike Tyson with the
author (top), Michael Bentt (below left) and George
Foreman all raise a smile*

It was his very last amateur fight for which he will always be remembered – a memory he still treasures himself beyond all others in the ring. For it was in the long, hot Mexican summer of 1968 that he became Britain's last Olympic boxing champion. 'It's amazing to think we haven't had another for nearly 30 years. In a way I'll be sad when somebody else wins a gold medal, because I'm proud to have held the record for so long. Yet amateur boxing in this country needs someone to give the old game a lift,' he says.

Finnegan was 24 years old when he travelled to Mexico City as part of a strong British team that included John H. Stracey, later to become world welterweight champion. 'I suppose I was getting on a bit for an amateur, but I'd had three and a half years out of the ring from the time I was 16,' he explained. 'I got myself a brand new motor bike, so it was the bike and birds for me. I forgot all about boxing for a while.'

He reckons the break worked to his advantage. 'I'd been boxing for as long as I can remember. Terry used to have me and Kevin sparring out in the garden as soon as we were old enough to walk. I joined Hayes Amateur Boxing Club as soon as I was old enough – a fellah called Dickie Gunn, who sadly passed away just recently, used to train us. He was great, but I think he was a bit upset when I left him. But I still kept fit carrying all those bricks on the building sites and I bumped into him again when I was nearly 20. He told me he had a couple of good young kids in the gym who would give me a lesson – and that got me going. I went back and sorted the kids out – and I found I was really enjoying myself again.'

Finnegan went on to claim his first national ABA title within a year and had become an experienced international by the time he arrived at the Olympic village in Mexico City. 'I was feeling 100 per cent fit, too, rarin' to go,' he said. 'I'd left home and was living in a caravan at the time, but I made sure I ate all the right food, all good English stuff, steak and the like. And David James, who was in charge of the boxing team, had introduced us to circuit training at Crystal Palace for the first time. Without sounding flash, I really fancied my chances of at least getting a medal of some sort.

'Even the heat and the altitude didn't bother me much. I had a nice easy fight in the first round, against some guy from Tanzania. I think I could have knocked him out, but I stayed the three rounds to get a good feel of the ring and the arena.' His programme grew a whole lot tougher after that, however. He had to overcome a powerful German in the second round, then had to draw on all his reserves of skill and courage to fight his way past Yugoslav Mate Parlov – later to become a professional world champion – in the quarter-final.

'At least I knew I had a medal now. But I was starting to dream that maybe it could be a gold one,' said Finnegan. 'In the semi-final I had to fight an American called Alfred Jones, who had been strongly fancied to win the title. He was a smart, tough guy, but I managed to outbox him. And there I was in the final! I had a bloke from Russia called Alexi Kiselev to beat now – and I knew he was going to be the hardest fight of all. In those days, you could guarantee that a fighter from Russia was a tough sonofabitch. He had knocked out the Mexican challenger in the semi-final, so I knew he could punch. Mind, he didn't do himself any favours – the crowd hated him after that! And in those days nobody liked the Russians much anyway.'

But while the Mexican crowd were firmly on his side, Finnegan still plotted a cautious strategy for the final. 'I knew that Kiselev had a big punch. I also knew that in the previous Olympics, four years before, he had reached the semi-finals – as a light heavyweight. The fact he had come down a weight to middleweight told me that he might have had to sweat off a few pounds to make the limit. And that would mean he could have stamina problems,' he said. 'So my plan was just to be patient and mobile for that opening round, make him work hard and use up that energy. I was ready to lose the round if necessary. Then I would step up the pace for the remaining two rounds.'

It was a plan that worked to near perfection. Kiselev, a powerful, purposeful but basically one-paced performer, threw more punches and had slightly the better of the first round, against an opponent who was quite content to back-pedal and make him chase after him. Then Finnegan suddenly unleashed his own attacking powers in round two, prepared to take on the Russian at his own game. It was a thrilling round – but Finnegan was unsure as he walked back to his corner at the bell whether he had landed enough punches to have sneaked it. 'I knew, basically, that it was all on the final round,' he said. 'I just had to go out there and give it all I had.' Kiselev must have harboured identical doubts, because the two fighters punched themselves almost to exhaustion in that thrilling last three minutes. 'When I got back to my corner, they were all jubilant – but I still didn't know if I had won,' said Finnegan. 'I believed I had just about nicked it, but in amateur boxing in those days, with all the politics involved, you just never knew what to expect.' Then, after an agonising delay while the scorecards of the five judges were counted, came the result: 'The 1968 Olympic middleweight champion, by a majority of three votes to two – CHRIS FINNEGAN of Great Britain!'

It was as desperately close as that. But Finnegan didn't care. 'It was the proudest moment you could ever imagine, especially a few minutes later when I stood on the podium to receive my gold medal and they played the national anthem. I thought of all the folks back home. I knew it was about four o'clock in the morning back in Britain, but I knew there would be a lot of people back there, rubbing their eyes but almost as proud as I was,' he said. 'If you could bottle the way I felt there and then, you could sell it for a fortune.' After a night or two of celebration at the Olympic village, Finnegan was fêted when he arrived back in London as Britain's newest sporting hero.

'They took me to Pinewood Studios for an official reception and I had bigwigs all over the place coming up and shaking my hand. I was on the television, in the newspapers – it was amazing,' he said. 'But the biggest honour of all came a few months later when I was told I was being awarded the MBE by the Queen. Going to Buckingham Palace . . . now that really was something for a kid who had spent most of his life on the building sites.

'But the day I got it was almost a disaster. I'd turned pro by then and had my first six-rounder the night before I was due at the Palace. A tough one it was too – I had a big split right down my nose and half a dozen stitches in a cut over my eye. Of course there had to be a tube strike on the day, so I couldn't get to the Palace by underground – and all the taxis were busy. I think I ran most of the way, but I was still about an hour and a half late by the time I got there. And the stitches over my eye had opened up as well, so I was having to mop the blood away.

'When I finally got inside, this posh geezer stopped me and asked me where did I think I was going. "I've come to pick up a gong, mate," I told him. He looked at me as if I was a nutter. Then he must have recognised my nose! "By heck, you're Chris Finnegan," he said. He got me inside pretty sharp. Luckily I'd only missed the rehearsals, so they just told me quickly that when it was my turn to meet the Queen I had to take three paces forward, then bow or curtsey or whatever it was. And I must not open my mouth to talk to her unless she talked to me first.

'But when it finally was my turn, she was brilliant. "I hear you had a very difficult time last night," she said, gazing at my wounds. I muttered something in reply, then she really surprised me. "I was so thrilled when you won your medal. I stayed up and watched you all the way through the Olympics," she said. I was sold hook, line and sinker on Her Majesty from that moment on. I know she's had a pretty tough time of it lately, but I think she's wonderful. I hope she goes on forever.'

Dynamite in his Gloves –
Jelly in his Legs

George Foreman v Joe Frazier

George Foreman was born in Marshall, Texas, on 10 January 1949. He climaxed a brilliant amateur career by winning the gold medal in the heavyweight division at the 1968 Olympic Games in Mexico. He won the world heavyweight championship for the first time by stopping Joe Frazier in 1973. After losing the title to Muhammad Ali the following year he eventually retired in 1977, but made a remarkable comeback ten years later that culminated with him regaining the WBA and IBF portions of the title by knocking out Michael Moorer in 1994. At 45 he became the oldest man to win the title.

GEORGE FOREMAN was the most awesome punching-machine in the world . . . and the most feared. It was 22 January 1973 and Foreman, just past his 24th birthday, was at the absolute peak of his career as he prepared to challenge for the world heavyweight title. He had served notice of his ferocious pedigree by smashing aside all before him to win the gold medal for America in the Mexico City Olympics five years previously. Since turning professional in 1969, he had continued on that same barnstorming trail. His record revealed his power – 37 fights, 37 victories. Twenty-seven of his opponents had failed to last beyond three rounds. Only three had managed to keep running long enough and fast enough to survive the distance.

At 6ft 4ins he was a colossus. Joe Frazier, the champion he faced that night in Kingston, Jamaica, was a good four inches shorter.

Foreman was taller, he outweighed him, he outreached him and he outpunched him. So why on earth were the challenger's knees trembling as he made his unsteady way to the ring? 'I was so scared I was uncontrollable,' he freely admits now. 'I never ever wanted to get in the same ring as this guy. I guess I was in awe of him.

'I had this fear inside me right from the time the fight was made – maybe even before that. Smokin' Joe – he didn't get that name for nothing. This is one of the greatest fighters of all time. I'd seen Joe Frazier beat up on guys like Muhammad Ali, Jerry Quarry and Buster Mathis. They'd hit him with everything and he'd only gain strength form it. Mathis mopped up the ring with him for nine rounds, then Joe knocked him out in the tenth. Quarry hit him with everything one round – and when Joe walked back to his corner at the bell he was GRINNING! How d'you fight a guy like that? If you hit him he likes it. And if you don't hit him he gets mad! Wow, he'd even knocked Ali down.'

Frazier, four years older than Foreman, had indeed established a fearsome reputation, with ten successful world title fights already behind him. He had won the vacant title after Ali had been banned from the ring for refusing to enlist in the US Army at the height of the war in Vietnam. Only the rugged Argentinian Oscar Bonevena had been able to survive against him before Ali had returned to challenge him for his old crown. When Frazier outpointed Ali, knocking him down in the 15th round, he became a hero of white America. Ali was reviled by millions of Americans at that time for his stand against the establishment.

Foreman had his own moment in the political spotlight when he won his Olympic medal. Those games became notorious for the Black Power salute of medal-winning athletes Tommie Smith and John Carlos which outraged white America. When Foreman struck gold, he pulled out a tiny American flag which he waved proudly in the ring. 'It wasn't no political gesture against the other guys. I was just so proud that moment of being an American,' he said. Nevertheless, it made him enemies among his own black countrymen.

That was five years before. Right now Frazier was the only thing on his mind, haunting his head. 'I always wanted to fight for the title one day. But I hoped that by the time I was ready Joe Frazier and Muhammad Ali would have both retired!' he says. 'I hoped for an easier route.' Foreman had also begun to distrust his manager and trainer Dick Sadler in the past few months. So while Sadler remained his manager, he brought in the universally respected former world light heavyweight champion Archie Moore to supervise his training. Foreman, for all his ferocity, had never totally believed in himself. The unloved former champion Sonny Liston, whose malevolent, scowling presence was as intimidating as his destructive fists, had once told him: 'You gotta look mean as well as be mean in this game.'

Foreman had taken the message to heart, hence the menacing look, the belligerent image he'd learned to cultivate. Now Moore worked on redoubling the bad-man inside the challenger, building up a real and all-consuming hatred for the champion. 'When you see Frazier, you look him in the eye. Don't you move a muscle until his eyes leave you,' he would constantly tell Foreman. 'By the time Archie had finished I'd never channelled so much hate. That's what he thought you needed to be the champ. I didn't even dislike Joe Frazier, but at the weigh-in I stared at him with cold, hard eyes, trying to establish a dominance over him.'

It was Frazier who eventually broke away. But then he strode angrily across to Foreman, pushed into him and warned: 'I should kill you right now.' It set the tone for genuine ill-feeling between the two by the time they came together for real, in the ring. Foreman, as challenger, was first to make his entrance. 'As I walked down the aisle and up the stairs into the ring my knees were quaking with fear,' he said. 'I had to start dancing around the ring because if I stood still everyone would have noticed the Jello in my legs – and maybe they'd have cancelled the fight, figuring nobody that terrified should be fighting!'

Frazier made his entrance to tumultuous applause. And Moore started yelling at Foreman: 'Look at him! You look right in his eyes! You look right there!' Foreman takes up the story: 'My knees barely carried me to the centre of the ring for the referee's instructions. I was stomping the floor to try to keep them from shaking. I found his eyes and kept staring at them. I was only hoping he wouldn't look down because he'd see my legs were trembling. I kept telling myself not to be scared, but the knees didn't listen. The strange thing was, though, that despite all the fear I still believed I was gonna be the new champion. I told myself I wasn't gonna let him hurt me. I was gonna hurt him first.'

That wasn't how it happened though. It was Frazier who landed the first telling punch of the fight, his favourite lunging left hook which thudded into the side of Foreman's face – maybe waking him up. Frazier, as always, was boring his way forward throughout the opening round. But he was playing into the challenger's hands. 'Seldom did I meet a guy who was chasing me. But Joe Frazier was in my face all the time. This was awful comfortable for me. I had problems with guys who would run,' he said.

Foreman jabbed his left hand out constantly at the crouching, marauding Frazier. Then, towards the end of the round, he let go with his own favourite punch, a right uppercut that had devastated many an opponent in the past. This one was a beauty, crunching into Frazier's chin. And down the champion went, staggering up at the count of eight. 'I was surprised – and worried,' said Foreman. 'When Joe Frazier goes down, that's when he gets mad. But for three years I'd focused on how to finish a man when he was hurt. I hit him with another uppercut and down he went again.' Frazier, never lacking in courage, climbed up a second time, only to be driven over yet again as the bell came to his temporary rescue.

'It wasn't until that third knockdown that I realised Joe was in serious trouble. He was still in distress when we came out for the second round. I put him down again with another right hand, then a fifth time. Then I looked over at Yank Durham, in Frazier's corner, hoping he would stop the fight. Joe was stumbling badly. But his corner made no move to stop it. I started thinking that the only way I was gonna stop this warrior was to kill him, unless someone else stepped in on his behalf,' said Foreman.

For the fifth time, Frazier somehow found the instinct to lift himself back up. But the last punch of the slaughter, a booming right uppercut, sent him off his feet and into the air before he landed on his backside. This time, to the relief of everyone, referee Arthur Mercante finally called a halt. 'It was a pity it was allowed to go on for so long, but maybe people felt I might eventually tire and Joe would do to me what he'd done to so many others,' said Foreman, adding a heartfelt tribute to his stricken foe: 'This guy's one of the bravest of the brave. He'll go down in the hall of fame. He'd already earned millions, he had nothing to keep getting up off the canvas for. But he still gave it all he had – and then some. You have to respect him as a true warrior.'

The Foreman legend, of course, was only just beginning. He would lose his title to Ali in that astonishing Rumble in the Jungle in Zaire 21 months later, retire from boxing in 1977 to become a preacher – then launch his incredible comeback a full ten years later to help pay for his church funds. That second coming had its own heart-stopping conclusion when he knocked out Michael Moorer in Las Vegas in 1994 to regain the WBA and IBF portions of the world title. It guaranteed his immortality in the annals of sporting fame, as well as making him an instant hero to every middle-aged American who ever dreamed of recapturing his youth. 'I look back at the first George Foreman now and realise he was a guy in personal torment, he didn't have God or true friends to help him through his life the way I do now,' he says. 'But as a fighter – well, this ol' George Foreman here now wouldn't want to fight him!'

Desert Storm

Marvin Hagler v Thomas Hearns

Marvin Hagler was born in Newark, New Jersey, on 23 May 1954. He was the eldest of seven children brought up by his mother Mae, who took her family to Brockton, Massachusetts, when Marvin was 14 years old. He turned professional five years later and eventually won the undisputed world middleweight title in 1980, beating Britain's Alan Minter in London. He successfully defended the title a dozen times in a seven-year reign, before losing a highly controversial points decision to Sugar Ray Leonard in 1987. He retired after that fight and moved to Italy, where he has embarked on a second successful career as an actor in action films.

THE EXPLOSIVE OPENING ROUND between Marvin Hagler and Thomas Hearns, in Las Vegas on 15 April 1985, is still revered by many as the greatest three minutes in boxing history. It truly was as savagely compelling as any round could be: two proud and mighty warriors, two bitter rivals both blessed with devastating punching power – and neither prepared to take a backward step, such was the burning intensity of that rivalry. 'I felt like I had a monster inside me,' said Hagler. So what provoked such rage in a champion who, outside the ring, was as affable and kindly a man as you would ever meet? 'We had to travel round the country, visiting 21 cities, to publicise the fight. And Tommy just got me real angry, he just kept bad-mouthing me all the time,' answers Hagler. 'He kept repeating the same line: "I'm gonna knock your bald head all over the wall." I just used to laugh back at him and say, "Hey, that means you're really gonna show up!" But deep down I was mad.'

There may have been an even deeper, more enduring determination, though, hidden way back in the darkest corner of Hagler's mind, perhaps so far back it barely reached beyond his own subconscious. For Hagler, the undisputed middleweight champion of the world for the past five years, still felt like a man in the shadows. Ten successful defences of the crown he plundered from Britain's Alan Minter on a night when disgraceful crowd violence scarred his triumph had earned him millions of dollars. He was the hero of blue-collar America, the guy who'd had to succeed the hard way because he did not launch his career with all the benefits of big-time promoters behind him. Born into a Newark, New Jersey ghetto, the eldest of seven children, with only his mother Mae to bring them up, he had known real poverty in his childhood. The family moved to join relatives in Brockton, Massachusetts, in 1968 after race riots had torn apart their home town. Brockton was the birthplace of the fabled Rocky Marciano, former unbeaten world heavyweight champion, but it was now a long way from boxing's mainstream. The teenage Hagler joined forces with the Petronelli brothers, Pat and Goody, who ran a homely little gym in the town and, after his first manager was tragically killed in a car crash, the two brothers organised his career. They had come a long way together by the time Hagler prepared to defend his title against Hearns, former WBA world welterweight champion and the current WBC world light middleweight king. But still Hagler felt that while the working classes who eagerly bought up the cheap seats to cheer him recognised his greatness, he had yet to convince the cognoscenti, those in the $1,000 seats, the boxing press and those with power and influence.

This was the fight to prove his stature to the whole world. Hearns was already the darling of the media, and while he was moving up a division, there were many shrewd observers who felt Hearns's advantages in height – he was a beanpole 6ft 2ins – and reach would enable him to outfox and outbox the squat and much shorter champion. 'I knew how tough it would be. That's why I was two and a half months in training. No women, early to bed, running every morning. I was super-fit.

'And I was ready for a long night. I thought I would have to take my time and be patient because he would try to box his way through the fight.' But instead Hearns, whose stamina was always suspect, swept from his corner like a hurricane at the first bell. 'I was surprised – but delighted,' said Hagler. 'This was just the fight I wanted; he was playing right into my hands.' Two crunching right hands smashed into Hagler's face inside the opening 30 seconds. The second certainly seemed to shake him, although he insists, 'That's when I just knew I was gonna win. I thought to myself, "Now I know you got nuthin' worse". I was ready to gobble up everything he could throw and just keep on coming.'

With Hearns equally determined to stay his ground, the two stood toe to toe blasting punches at each other in an almost primitive exhibition of brute strength and courage. Something had to give – and suddenly blood began pouring from a cut on Hagler's forehead, thankfully in between his eyes. 'I didn't believe I was bleeding till they wiped it away in the corner. I don't know how it happened, but it wasn't a punch. Maybe we bumped heads,' he said. It didn't prevent him staggering Hearns with a right-hand piledriver right on the bell. And the stare of pure malevolence he gave Hearns as the round ended must have added to the challenger's discomfort.

No sequel could ever quite match the unbridled ferocity of that opening round, but round two came pretty close. Hearns was having increasing trouble dealing with Hagler's southpaw stance and stumbled over the champion's right foot several times. He was trying to use his extra reach and mobility to keep Hagler at bay, but it was an increasingly vain struggle. 'I was fighting the perfect fight. My combinations were coming off, my hand speed was good. And I was staying in so tight on him I could smell what he had for dinner!' said Hagler. As the round neared its close, Hearns was already beginning to look weary. And yet another pulverising left hook from Hagler sent him crashing to the floor. He climbed dazedly up, only to be battered against the ropes by a fusillade of punches. The bell brought temporary respite. But there was still just one glimmer of a chance for him – the cut had opened again on Hagler's forehead, and for a few frozen seconds in round three it almost spelled disaster for the champion. Referee Richard Steele stopped the contest to ask a ringside doctor whether the cut was too severe for him to continue. 'The doctor said, "Can you see?" I said, "Well, I ain't missin' him with my punches!" So he let me continue. I knew already in that round that I had him. He hit me with one good shot, but I was saying to him, "You got nothing". I was so close to him I had my head on his chest. And every time I give him a good shot, I could hear him wince. That told me I got this guy good. But the referee kept pushing me away, giving Tommy time to recover. Then there was the business with the eye. That all just made me madder and madder. Now I wanted to kill Tommy.'

Hearns was paying an increasingly heavy price for Hagler's anger. He was already looking like a man with nothing left to offer when a hard right hand landed on his temple, sending him spinning, open-mouthed, across the ring. Hagler rushed ruthlessly after him, landing two more right hands and then a sweeping left which sent Hearns tumbling. 'I wanted him to get up, because I'm not finished with him yet. He was such a big-mouth before the fight. I stood in the corner watching him, thinking, "If they let him carry on I'm gonna kill the guy". You have to have that type of instinct inside you to reach the top. You know the other guy is trying to take something away from you. You have to stop him, no matter how bad it hurts.' Hearns did climb courageously to his feet at the count of eight, trying to raise his hands to continue. But referee Steele mercifully stopped a gripping contest from ending in a slaughter of a brave man.

'When I look back now on how the fight was stopped, I'm happy. Because I have a great respect for Tommy now. He was a very brave man that night,' says Hagler. And the champion's sensational performance had already achieved the reward he most cherished – the adulation of all the sporting world. The capacity audience at Caesars Palace gave him a tumultuous ovation – once they had managed to catch their breath! He became a national celebrity in a country captivated by his indomitable courage and will to win.

Hagler's career ended two years later when he finally lost his world title to another arch-rival, Sugar Ray Leonard. The split decision points verdict to Leonard was, in the eyes of the vast majority of us at ringside, a gross injustice to a great champion. Ironically, Leonard, once the darling of the ring, is the man who suffered the long-term effects of that verdict most. He gets nothing more than a polite murmur of applause – accompanied by as many jeers – whenever he is introduced at ringside. Hagler, the blue-collar champion, the idol of the masses, is greeted like a triumphant emperor. His greatness won semi-official recognition when he was named Fighter of the '80s by America's prestigious *Boxing Illustrated* magazine, ahead of the likes of Leonard, Hearns and Mike Tyson. Nowadays he is a contented man indulging in new fantasies as a film actor in Italy. 'Mostly tough-guy roles,' he says. 'You have to learn to be patient, to sit and wait. But it's good fun. And what I like about it most is – you don't get punched . . .'

A New Prince is Crowned in Wales

Naseem Hamed v Steve Robinson

Naseem Hamed was born in Sheffield on 12 February 1974, the son of immigrant parents from the Yemen. Five times National Schoolboy Champion and twice Junior ABA Champion, he turned professional in 1992 and captured the European bantamweight title two years later. He then won the WBC international super-bantamweight title before moving up to featherweight to win the WBO world title from Steve Robinson in Cardiff in 1995.

IT WAS FIVE O'CLOCK in the morning and Naseem Hamed was enjoying himself hugely, sitting up with a crowd of friends in the foyer of the swank hotel just off the M4 near Newport. 'I guess I'd better go and get a few hours' sleep,' he told them eventually. 'After all, I'm fighting for the world title in about 16 hours time!'

Fighters are a breed apart, but few come with more bizarre credentials than the self-styled Prince from Sheffield. 'I actually stayed up all night before one fight, went to bed for a few hours' rest about two o'clock in the afternoon. What's wrong with that? It certainly hasn't done me any harm in my career. You sleep when you're tired.' Naseem's manager, mentor and trainer, Brendan Ingle, can bear testimony to those words. His precocious charge has often summoned him from his bed at two a.m. to go training in the homely gymnasium round the corner from Ingle's home. Naseem has been known also to take a plateful of sandwiches to his dressing-room a couple of hours before a fight, an idea that would make most fighters choke. You get hit in the belly and the whole lot will come up, is their argument. 'When I'm hungry I eat. When I'm tired I go to bed,' is his response. As he sat with his pals, awaiting his date with destiny in the formidable shape of WBO world featherweight champion Steve Robinson, his forthright convictions were difficult to challenge. After all, they had helped him to the brink of his ambition. The next day, or rather later that evening, he would have reached the goal that is every fighter's dream.

So what kept him awake? Was it nervous apprehension? Was the occasion getting to him? 'You must be joking!' he says. 'I was up late because I was happy, enjoying the company. I never had a nerve in my body leading up to that fight. In fact, I have never suffered nerves before any fight. Only the feeling of excitement, that all the hard work in the gym is about to bear fruit. I knew I had trained with total dedication, I was 1,000 per cent fit – and raring to go. And I knew, even then, that I would win, that I would be crowned champion. I never had a moment's doubt. That's not just trying to sound clever, that's me being totally honest.'

Naseem was set to challenge Robinson before the champion's highly vocal and partisan home supporters at the Cardiff Rugby Club ground on 30 September 1995. It was a risky decision by promoter Frank Warren to stage the fight outdoors so late into the autumn. The drizzling rain was hardly the ideal backcloth to a fight so eagerly anticipated throughout the whole of Britain – and in Wales in particular.

In an acrimonious build-up to the contest, the precocious Prince had angered Robinson's followers with his constant taunting of the champion and the message he had consistently trumpeted: I will knock out Robinson to win the title – there is no question, no doubt about it. Robinson's camp had also been embroiled in a bitter pre-fight war with promoter Warren, who had insisted the contest must go ahead on the scheduled date – even though it meant the champion had to cut short his honeymoon to begin his training.

The wrangle had been well publicised, which added fuel to the fervour of Robinson's supporters. And what a crowd turned up in the rain to cheer for their man. The stadium was crammed full, with more than 16,000 people defying the elements to give the challenger a frenzied taste of their bitterness towards him as he entered the ring first. 'People were spitting at me, I was hit by a coin thrown by one lunatic. And I could hear all the howls and the booing. But it didn't frighten me at all,' said Naseem. 'In fact, it was the opposite. It made me more determined than ever to win, just to ram it down their throats. I thought it was appalling the way they were acting towards me.'

Robinson, naturally, was given a hero's welcome as he bobbed his way from the dressing-room to the ring. Despite his tribulations he seemed in good heart, breaking that normally impassive expression to raise a smile of confidence in the direction of his fans after he climbed through the ropes. And confident he was entitled to be. After all, he had retained the title no fewer than seven times – and all before his own folk in Cardiff – since he captured the belt two and a half years previously. Naseem may have had a big mouth, but he was only a little man – only a jumped-up bantamweight who had never even fought as a featherweight before. 'Don't fall for his tricks, don't let him psyche you out of it. Don't let your guard drop, let him wear himself out with his dancing. Be patient – and the opening will come.' It was the message that the champion was repeating to himself over and over as they went through the preliminaries and in the opening round Robinson was as good as his words.

He kept his gloves high, protecting his chin. He stayed cool as the challenger pranced in front of him and he launched a few attacking sorties of his own, clipping Naseem if hardly hurting him. He had just about achieved enough to have shaved that opening round. It was to be the only time in the fight, however, when it resembled an even contest. For Naseem had found his bearings by the end of that first three minutes. He had warmed up in the chill dampness. Now he was ready to step up into a gear far beyond anything the champion could muster.

'I just went to town,' he said. 'I was really beginning to enjoy myself, having got to terms with the conditions.' From the start of the second round, Robinson must have felt like a man trying to stop a windmill. Naseem is a freak of the ring, a fighter who defies all the textbooks. He shimmied and he danced around the champion, he dropped his hands and thrust forward his chin, attempting to goad him. He grinned at Robinson, he taunted him into losing control. And when Robinson, like an enraged bull, fell for the antics and charged forward, he was smashed unmercifully by punches that rained in from the most improbable and sometimes outrageous angles. Naseem often seemed to leave his own chin totally exposed as he threw his own punches. But so lightning fast were his reactions that Robinson never had the opportunity to take advantage. Nobody could doubt his courage. But it produced only a fearful beating. As the rounds went by and his face began to show the bruises and the swellings caused by his challenger's punishment, the crowd, who had been hushed since the first round, tried to lift him. 'Robinson! Robinson! Robinson!' they chanted. Naseem heard it – and started to join in! 'I was just enjoying myself so much. And I wanted to pay back the crowd for the way they had treated me,' he said.

While people had questioned the power of Naseem's punches against a bigger opponent, he had been sparring with much larger fighters at Ingle's gym almost from the time he first turned up there as a nine-year-old urchin who wanted to learn to defend himself against racial abuse at school. 'A featherweight was nothing for Naz. He often spars with middleweights and even light heavyweights. And he hurts them, too, with his power,' said Ingle. Robinson was bearing painful testimony to those words as the beating continued relentlessly. As he tried manfully to press himself forward, only to find his opponent had performed his artful dodger act again, the words of an earlier Naseem opponent, Freddie Cruz from the Dominican Republic, sprung to mind. Cruz was a tough, durable character who had taken Robinson the full dozen rounds in a challenge for his title, but had later been obliterated inside six rounds by Naseem. 'I came to fight a man, not a boy,' he had scoffed when he first set eyes on his urchin-like opponent. But his opinions had changed somewhat after the opening round. 'Why aren't you hitting him back?' his frustrated cornerman asked him as he sunk, wide-eyed, on to his stool. 'I don't know where he is!' gasped Cruz.

Robinson was enduring the same nightmare. The first tangible sign that his resistance was beginning to evaporate came in the fifth round, when he was sent crashing to the canvas by a lightning four-punch combination, ended by a perfect right uppercut. He climbed to his feet and summoned all his strength to survive the round. It was merely a case of prolonging the agony. Naseem forced him to take heavy punishment for two more rounds. Then, in the eighth round, with Robinson by now looking a forlorn, desperate figure, the end came. Fittingly it was a punch you will not find in any textbook which did the damage. Naseem suddenly lunged forward and, so it seemed, totally off balance, threw a lunging left hook right into Robinson's face. He collapsed, semi-conscious and utterly exhausted, as the new champion celebrated above him. In defeat Robinson was magnanimous. 'You punch harder than anyone else I've ever fought,' he told Naseem. 'He was just unlucky to run into me,' says Naseem. 'He could have held the title a long time against ordinary challengers. But he couldn't take the power of my punches. That's no disgrace for him. Nobody can . . .'

Rock 'n' Roll in Motown

Thomas Hearns v Dennis Andries

Thomas Hearns was born in Memphis, Tennessee, on 18 October 1958. He moved to Detroit as a teenager to pursue his professional career and became the most successful member of the famous Kronk Gym. He won versions of a world title in every division from welterweight to cruiserweight – six altogether. That is a feat unequalled in boxing history.

EVEN IN AN ERA when the proliferation of weight divisions and world governing bodies combined to make the task of gathering titles somewhat less of an awesome achievement than it used to be, the record of Thomas Hearns still commands total respect. The world title trail blazed by the fabled Hit Man from Detroit stretches 14 years and half a dozen different weight divisions – welterweight, light middleweight, middleweight, super middleweight, light heavyweight and cruiserweight. That is a range of more than three stone – a phenomenal achievement.

Hearns had the advantages of height – at 6ft 2ins he was a beanpole in his welterweight days: it is amazing, when you see him now, to believe he could ever fit that frame into the 10 stone 7lbs limit – and explosive punching power which had its devastating effect even on opponents who, by nature, were much stronger than him. He was also a fast and elusive boxer when the needs demanded, and the combination of brute strength and artistry carried him to marvellous victories over great champions like Roberto Duran, Wilfred Benitez, Pipino Ceuvas and Virgil Hill.

Perhaps he gained even more acclaim from dramatic contests he lost, despite playing a noble role, to those other legendary names of the '80s, Marvin Hagler and Sugar Ray Leonard.

His record – more than 20 world title fights – is laced with illustrious names, sensational fights against the greatest warriors of his time. Yet the contest he will always regard as his greatest triumph was against an Englishman, Dennis Andries. It took place in Detroit – Hearns's adopted city – on 7 March 1987. 'And it was so memorable because it was the biggest mountain I ever had to climb,' says this soft-talking son of the south – Hearns was born in Memphis, Tennessee, moving to the motor city when Emmanuel Steward, founder of the legendary Kronk Gym, spotted his potential and signed him into the professional ranks. It was a move which perfectly suited both men. Steward at that time, in the late 1970s, was just beginning to build his reputation. He needed a headliner in his team to win national and international prominence. Hearns, of the easy-going southern nature, was toughened up, mentally and physically, by the poundings he took daily in a gym whose reputation as the hardest schooling place in the boxing world is no mere myth. Tommy got hurt – and learned to hurt back.

Hearns was still only 21 when he won his first crown, stopping the Mexican Pipino Cuevas – a noted puncher himself – inside two rounds to win the WBA welterweight title. He outpointed Wilfred Benitez to plunder the WBC light middleweight championship some 16 months later, but had failed to take the undisputed middleweight title from Marvin Hagler, being stopped in the third round of a bloody and brutal battle. He kept his hold on the light middleweight title, but the defeat by Hagler had already raised the question throughout boxing – was his current division his limit? It was a question which raised doubts in his own mind, which made him stop and think carefully when manager Steward came to him with the offer to face Andries for the WBC world light heavyweight title.

Andries at that time was barely known in America, but he had outpointed an American – J.B. Williamson – to win the title the previous year. The new champion was not noted as a devastating puncher or a craftsman – but he was strong, brave and remorseless. He was also more than a stone heavier than Hagler, himself the heaviest man Hearns had so far faced.

'I also had other problems,' recalled Hearns. 'I was suffering a lot of trouble with my hands, like a lot of hard punchers do. And I was getting this sinus problem as well. But I decided I had to take the challenge. My feeling is that we all have problems to face in our lives. It's a matter of being strong enough to deal with them. If you feel in your heart you can accomplish something, go out there and do it. So I stuffed myself up, pumped myself up, to build up the extra weight. I was stuffed full of food – and my stomach showed it. Even then, I still weighed in with my clothes on and pennies in my pockets. The irony was that at the weigh-in I was actually a quarter of a pound heavier than he was!'

Andries had made a big play about his natural weight advantage when the two had come face to face before the fight, claiming Hearns lacked the power to hurt an opponent of his size and strength. His record suggested he was right. Although Andries had been regarded as only a journeyman in his early fighting days, when he was beaten several times, the only man to knock him out was a full-blown heavyweight, former British champion Dave Pearce. 'You'll have to bring out that gun to hurt me,' Andries had taunted Hearns who, as a police reserve officer in his spare time, carried firearms on duty.

Andries was to discover painfully the false bravado of his words as early as the second round when Hearns sent him staggering with a sharp right hand. It was already apparent that Tommy, the taller man by a good three inches, was also sharper on his feet and possessed the kind of hand speed which Andries had never experienced before. But there was trouble for the challenger in that round as well, when a clash of heads left blood trickling from a cut near the corner of his left eye. Hearns protested, but referee Isaac Herrera – at 65 surely one of the oldest men ever to officiate at a world title fight – saw nothing amiss.

'I don't think it was deliberate on Dennis's part, just awkwardness. But it showed me I had to be careful, I had to take my time, not get drawn into close-quarter stuff,' said Hearns. For most of the third round Hearns stuck to his game plan, peppering Andries's face with his left jab and using his long legs to keep out of harm's way. But then he suddenly unleashed two ferocious right hooks which sent the champion crashing to the floor. 'He showed how strong he was, by getting up. A lot of guys wouldn't have beaten the count,' said Hearns. It was, however, the first tangible sign of the slaughter that was about to unfold . . .

Andries managed to keep out of trouble for the next two rounds, although Hearns had already established a commanding lead as they came together for round six. Then Tommy raised the pace and fury to a level way beyond the champion's grasp. A lightning right hook sent Andries tumbling for the second time in the fight. Although he climbed unsteadily to his feet as the count reached eight, he was clearly in distress. He was quickly bundled over again, then slipped over without a punch being thrown, then collapsed yet again from another fusillade of punches. Hearns's home-town crowd were screaming for him now, seeing the title that many of them felt was beyond him about to become his property. But Andries, in one of the most courageous displays of sheer bloody-minded defiance ever produced by a British fighter, was up yet again, grabbing Hearns round the waist, clutching, holding, doing anything to prevent the challenger from striking again. 'He was so strong that I could take nothing for granted,' said Hearns. 'My mind was telling me to stay in there, to stay focused and to be patient. Dennis made me fight. He made me use my head as well as my hands.'

Andries managed to remain on his feet for the next two rounds as Hearns took time to regain his strength. It has been known for boxers to punch themselves out against durable opponents, draining their own energy to such an extent that they have nothing left to offer in the later rounds of a gruelling fight. Hearns was determined not to suffer this fate. But in round nine he unleashed another crunching overhand right, sending Andries crashing to the floor once more. This time the champion, who by this stage must have been fighting on instinct alone, somersaulted straight back up. Hearns was taken by surprise as his foe suddenly lunged back at him and, as they wrestled, they both stumbled to the canvas.

Andries had one more shock for the challenger in round ten as he clipped him with a sharp left that left Hearns on his backside. But he was up before the count could begin – and this time Andries had nothing left to answer the bombardment that rained down on him. He went down once, hauled himself up – and promptly collapsed again before another punch could be thrown. Even the hard-nosed audience in America's toughest city was beseeching the referee to bring a merciful end to the massacre by this stage. As Andries picked himself up and, in his barely conscious state, headed unsteadily to a neutral corner, his brave defence was finally ended.

Hearns had sympathy for the deposed champion. 'He was a brave, brave man. I'm proud to think he later became my friend,' he said. 'But I was so thrilled because I had proved something to myself. And the crowd cheering was music to me. I enjoy making myself happy – but I enjoy making the people happy as well.'

The Angry Man's Revenge

Herbie Hide v Michael Bentt

Herbie Hide was born in Nigeria on 27 August 1971, but came to Britain as a two year old child and was brought up with an English family in Norwich. He turned professional in 1989, after reaching the ABA Heavyweight final earlier that year, and won the British title just over three years later. He became WBO world heavyweight champion in 1994, knocking out Michael Bentt in the seventh round, only to lose the title to Riddick Bowe in his first defence.

WHILE LENNOX LEWIS and Frank Bruno have rightfully been acclaimed for bringing back at least segments of the World Heavyweight title to Britain during the 1990s, after a gap of nearly 100 years, the achievements of Michael Bentt and Herbie Hide have passed largely unnoticed by the sporting world. The triumph of the London-born Bentt, who obliterated Tommy Morrison to win the WBO title, is dealt with in his own chapter. But when he agreed to face British champion Hide in his first defence, it set the scene for an historic encounter – and a bitter personal duel. The contest was arranged for 19 March 1994, at Millwall's spanking new football ground, The New Den, in South East London. While the 22-year-old challenger was born in Nigeria, he had lived in East Anglia since he was brought over, as a two-year-old child, to be brought up with an English couple. He was English enough to win the British title a year earlier. That meant nobody could deny this was a fight with an all-domestic cast as Bentt, despite his years in New York, had always retained his British passport.

The greater intrigue was whether Hide lacked the physical dimensions – he was just 13 stone 6lbs when he began his professional career in 1989 – and the mental stability needed to succeed at the higher levels. He had won all his previous 25 fights, all bar one inside the distance. But he was also known to possess an explosive temper on the end of a very short fuse. That fiery temperament had got him into trouble outside the ring. Could it be harnessed, controlled, to help rather than hinder his control inside the ring? Bentt, at 28 six years older, was a lovely, gentle man away from his sport, but crafty and ruthless enough to try and exploit Hide's questionable disposition when they were brought together in a five-star West End hotel to publicise the event. He cajoled the challenger as they were pushed shoulder to shoulder on the hotel verandah by photographers eager to capture some aggro in their pictures. The simmering tension between the two suddenly erupted into open violence as punches began to fly and photographers scattered as the pair grappled to the floor. Promoter Barry Hearn, who had not witnessed the outbreak of the violence, was able, with the help of several burly assistants, to eventually pull them apart. It was an ugly incident, a blot on boxing's image, and after the dramatic pictures made the front and back pages of the newspapers the next morning the British Boxing Board of Control acted quickly to fine both men heavily.

Hide, with some justification, claimed loud and long that he had been harangued into his actions. While his words provoked little public sympathy, the unsavoury episode had left its mark on him. 'From that day on, I was more determined than I have ever been in my life to win that fight,' he revealed. 'I was mad, I was angry. But in a funny way it took all the temper from me. I had more of what you would call a cold, calculating anger now. I knew that what Bentt was doing was trying to intimidate me, to have me scared of him even before we went into the ring together. But it had exactly the opposite effect. I was so determined, I was ready to die in that ring before letting him beat me. And I mean that, honestly.'

By the evening of the 'real' fight, Hide had been in training for ten weeks. 'The longest and hardest training I have ever done. I was in absolutely perfect condition. And I was weighing in at well over 15 stone, only about a stone lighter than him. I knew that most people had written me off because they said I wasn't big enough and I hadn't really beaten anybody who mattered. That didn't bother me at all. I was so totally focused on Bentt, after what had happened, that I knew, I just knew, there was no way I could lose. It's a strange feeling, but wonderful, simply KNOWING you are going to win a world title.'

While Bentt had shown awesome punching power in disposing of Tommy Morrison in barely half a round just five months earlier, there were questions about his stamina. Hide had his own reservations about the champion's ability to survive a dozen rounds at a blistering pace – and set his pre-fight plans accordingly. 'My aim was simple enough,' he says. 'I knew I was fitter than he was, I knew I was quicker as well. I didn't plan on running from him, but I wanted to keep the pace electric for the first half of the fight, tire him out – and then really take over.'

It was a blueprint that worked with almost uncanny accuracy. From the very start Hide came bustling out of his corner, not afraid to stand close to the bigger man and peppering his face with his much sharper jab. 'It was controlled agression,' says Hide. Bentt, who had laboured through his own training for the fight, looked distinctly uneasy by the end of the opening round. His face betrayed his growing frustration as Hide continued to dominate proceedings, growing in confidence sufficiently to really hurt him with some incisive, powerful punching – and all at high speed.

For speed was the key to Hide's success – the kind of pace that Bentt had never encountered before. By the sixth round, the halfway mark, the champion was a man in acute distress, able to do little more than paw away at the challenger who continued to torment him without mercy. Bentt had nothing left to offer – and he was knocked out by a crisp combination in round seven. Hide had triumphed against all odds – now he was allowed his celebration in the ring. But his glory was cut short as Bentt collapsed in his dressing-room and had to be rushed to hospital where surgeons discovered a brain abnormality. He would never box again.

Hide was to lose his title in his very first defence, his quicksilver skills just not sufficient to offset the sheer bulk of American Riddick Bowe, who knocked him down seven times in five gruesome rounds in Las Vegas. But there was a heartwarming postscript to the vendetta between Hide and Bentt. 'While in Vegas I met Michael again. We chatted, had a few laughs together – and became firm friends,' says Herbie. 'He's become like an uncle to my brother Alan, who's nine years old. He sends him a present on his birthday and they write to each other regularly. Michael Bentt may have been a bit of a nutter as far as the build-up to his fight with me was concerned, but he's really a lovely man, as sweet a person as you'll ever meet.'

A High-flyer for Dignity

Evander Holyfield v Riddick Bowe

Evander Holyfield was born in Altmore, Alabama, on 19 October 1962,
but raised in Atlanta, Georgia, where his family moved when he was
three years old. He won a light heavyweight bronze medal in the 1984
Olympic Games in Los Angeles after being controversially disqualified in
his semi-final bout. He became an instant millionaire when he turned
professional, signing a four-year promotional contract worth £1.6 million.
He won his first world title – the WBA cruiserweight championship – in
only his 12th contest and by 1988 he had unified the title, adding the
WBC and IBF titles to his list. He then moved up to the heavyweight
division, where he knocked out Buster Douglas in the third round to
become the undisputed world champion in 1990. He lost the title to
Riddick Bowe two years later, but followed Floyd Patterson and
Muhammad Ali to become only the third man to regain the title by
outpointing Bowe in 1993.

BRAVERY AND BOXING go hand in hand. It takes a man of
special courage, far beyond the realms of most of us, to climb
through those ropes and into the ring, knowing there is an opponent
waiting there whose sole ambition is to hurt him, to separate his
mind from his body. No coward ever laced a pair of boxing gloves.
But even at this rarified level, there still exists degrees of courage
beyond the reach of all but a chosen, very special, few. Evander
Holyfield was blessed with such fortitude – he is the bravest fighter
I ever had the privilege of meeting and watching from ringside.

One would also struggle to find a champion of greater dignity than the softly spoken, impeccably mannered gentleman from America's deep south. If he was the ultimate warrior in the ring, he was also a great ambassador for a sport which desperately needed him back at the helm in the autumn of 1993. In November of the previous year Holyfield had lost his undisputed world heavyweight title to the brash New Yorker Riddick Bowe. It was a heroic performance even in defeat from Holyfield, who was outweighed by more than two stone but who still sought to stand toe to toe with a bully and slug it out, before being narrowly outpointed.

The first triumphant action by Bowe's manager Rock Newman was to aim a kick at a ringside photographer. It was an appalling indication of the tasteless reign to come. Bowe split the title by throwing his WBC belt into a dustbin rather than face Lennox Lewis, who had previously been promised the first challenge (Lewis, who had stopped Bowe to win the super-heavyweight Olympic gold medal in Seoul in 1988, became one of the few men to be awarded a world title outside the ring). Instead, Bowe knocked over a couple of hapless, outclassed veterans and, the invidious Newman at his side, embarked on a tasteless world tour which served only to further tarnish the title.

Holyfield, meanwhile, had announced his retirement soon after losing the title. Nobody begrudged him that. He was 30 years old, five years older than the new champion. He had already been through many wars in his 11 world title contests. He was the richest fighter the sport had yet produced, his earnings totalling a staggering $82 million (he would later become the first sportsman in history to pass the $100 million mark). And, in defeat by Bowe, he had gained the world's respect. For all his courage, Evander lacked one crucial element – size. He was just 12 stone 9lbs when he launched his professional career at the end of 1984. Even with the advice of dietary and body-building experts, he was still only 14 stone 12lbs when he won the heavyweight title – tiny in the modern era of giants. 'It ain't the size of the man, it's the size of the heart in the man that counts,' was his answer to those who doubted his physical strength. And that heart was now beating its own message to his mind: 'You can't quit boxing on a low note like this. You can still beat this guy.' Within a month, Holyfield had changed his mind and announced he was to fight again. 'I still have a clause in the contract with Bowe which gives me a rematch. And that's what I want,' he said.

Bowe and Newman eventually honoured their contract and the fight was set for Caesars Palace in Las Vegas on 6 November 1993

– 51 weeks after their first meeting. The champion anticipated a far less arduous battle this time. Holyfield had taken only one warm-up contest, a lacklustre points victory over Alex Stewart. 'He's a shot fighter,' was the Bowe–Newman verdict. A lot of neutral observers feared likewise. But it served to bring complacency into the camp of a champion whose outrageous eating binges had seen his weight soar to the 20-stone mark during his reign.

While Bowe's training was desultory, Holyfield worked ceaselessly to build up his body and his strength. He had a new trainer, Emmanuel Steward, head of the famed Kronk Gym in Detroit, to assist him this time – and Steward insisted that the path to victory lay in three square meals a day. By the time they weighed in Holyfield, his gleaming body still chiselled, was his heaviest ever – 15 stone 7lbs. Bowe's weight had gone up, too, from their last meeting – but his 17 stone 10lbs represented 11lbs of extra flab. 'His weight is up to him. All I know is that I'm ready,' said Holyfield. 'I fought a lousy fight the last time. I have to try again to prove to myself that I'm a better fighter than he is. And I guess I just kinda miss having that title. I'll enjoy it more the second time around.' The challenger was ready for anything – bar the astonishing scenes about to unfold at the 15,000-capacity outdoor arena two nights later.

Holyfield, as the challenger, was first to walk into the chill night air and into the ring, greeted by a roar of applause. Bowe's appearance brought a mixture of indifference and a few ragged jeers. There was no questioning the sympathies of a packed audience. But it was the champion who bounded from his corner at the first bell, to blast an overhand right which landed high on Holyfield's head, causing him to stagger backwards. Bowe, sensing a quick kill, charged forward throwing a fusillade of punches from both hands. For a tortured few seconds it seemed that Holyfield's great crusade would end in embarrassment, until he managed to pull himself away from the onslaught and harness his mind and body again.

It was to be one of the few backward steps he would take. While the massive champion used his potent jab to keep him at bay for the first three rounds, Holyfield was constantly probing for an opening. 'The idea wasn't to fight a defensive fight on the outside, but to get inside him, where his extra reach wouldn't count,' said Evander later. 'And I planned to wear him down, to keep the pace fast, to take away his strength.' He was quite content to let Bowe take the opening three rounds, but in round four his whole effort moved up several gears. Bowe was already beginning to tire, and as he did so his left hand began to drop lower. Holyfield began to hurt him with his own powerful overhand right, constantly forcing the champion backwards. It was a similar story in rounds five and six. And at the halfway stage Bowe was already a forlorn figure, blood seeping from cuts over the left eyebrow and on the bridge of his nose. He was breathing deeply, while Holyfield still looked as fresh as he had in the preliminaries.

It seemed that Holyfield was ready to blitz his way to victory when, after one minute and two seconds of round seven, came the most bizarre incident in the whole history of heavyweight boxing. Holyfield suddenly broke off from a clinch and walked away, staring uncomprehendingly into the darkened sky. He couldn't believe his own eyes. Hurtling towards the ring was a parachutist who crash-landed seconds later, hitting the apron of the ring and falling backwards into the crowd, his parachute entangled in the overhead lights. Chaos broke out as security guards sought to prevent the enraged crowd from attacking the invader, who was eventually released from the straps of his parachute and hustled away to a police cell. The lights above the ring were popping, leading many to believe it was gunfire. Several spectators had to be taken to hospital, suffering from minor injuries or shock, including Bowe's wife Judy, who was three months pregnant and had fainted when she thought her husband was being fired at.

It took 21 minutes for the parachute to be disentangled from the spotlights and order to be restored. The two fighters were both wrapped in dressing-gowns and blankets to keep their bodies as warm as possible in the by now cold air. There was no question that the enforced rest had been of more help to Bowe; it had allowed him to gain a second wind. But it was still Holyfield who dominated the seventh and eighth rounds, picking up his rhythm immediately, stifling Bowe's own attacks and peppering the champion with his counters.

Bowe, sensing his title was slipping away, now summoned the willpower to launch a despairing late challenge. If the challenger had dominated the middle rounds, he had to withstand a final three rounds of trench warfare. In the final round, especially, Bowe charged at him like an enraged bull, searching for the knockout he knew he needed. Yet, having withstood the savagery of that attack, Holyfield displayed those enormous reserves of strength and courage as he launched his own blistering counter-attack in the last minute. Such was the single-minded ferocity of both fighters that neither heard the final bell and they carried on hurling punches until they were eventually dragged apart.

It was close, but Holyfield was declared the victor on two judges' scorecards, with the third scoring it a draw. 'It was all down to determination, to desire,' said the new champion. 'And I wanted to prove people wrong. A lot of them said that I was washed up, that they feared for me if I went back into that ring again. I understood their concern, but it just made me all the more determined to show them that I could be champion again. I guess I like to do things that people think I can't.'

As for the lunatic intruder, Holyfield confessed: 'It was scary because I just didn't know what it was. Strange things cross your mind in moments like that. All I could think of was that girl who got stabbed on the tennis court.' But if the paraglidist thought he was pulling off one hell of a stunt, he was only kidding himself. Evander Holyfield was already proving that it was possible to fly without a motor strapped to his back. He was flying instead on the wings of a glorious dream.

One-way Traffic on the Boardwalk

Lloyd Honeyghan v Donald Curry

Lloyd Honeyghan was born in Jamaica on 22 April 1960. His family emigrated to Britain when he was nine years old and he was brought up in the London suburb of Bermondsey, where he still lives. Turning professional at the age of 20, Honeyghan captured the British, Commonwealth and European welterweight titles before achieving a totally unexpected victory over American Don Curry in Atlantic City in 1986 to become the undisputed world champion. He relinquished the WBA and IBF titles before losing the WBC title to Mexican Jorge Vaca in 1987. He regained the title from Vaca within five months but finally lost it to American Marlon Starling in 1989.

LLOYD HONEYGHAN pondered briefly on the question. 'My greatest memory? It has to be that night with Sheila. Or was it Gladys . . .?' Then he roared with laughter. 'You know me, man, I always had far more fun with the ladies than in the ring. I always preferred loving to fighting.' It was a classic answer from a man whose prowess with the ladies was legendary – he claims to have bedded at least a thousand, and I have no cause to doubt him. But Honeyghan in his prime was also one of the greatest fighters this country has ever produced, a champion whose heart was even bigger than his ego. And that ego, when it came to fighting talk, was something to behold. It needed to be when he travelled to America in the autumn of 1986 to challenge for the undisputed welterweight championship of the world. Don Curry, the champion, had earned the nickname of The Cobra: testimony to the venom which poured from his gloves as he thrashed every pretender to his crown. He was a magnificent fighting machine, his vicious punching prowess matched by his speed and elegance. He had already assumed the mantle of The Greatest Pound for Pound Fighter on Earth. And he seemed invincible.

Only a handful of British journalists crossed the Atlantic with Honeyghan, such was the overwhelming lack of belief in his chances, even among his own countrymen. To be bluntly honest, those of us who were present in Atlantic City on the night of 27 September were more fearful of his health than optimistic of seeing a sensation unfold. But the man himself had no shred of self-doubt. 'I'm just gonna go out there and bash him up. He's made for me. And he's mine. I haven't come all the way over here to look at that ocean and then fall down when he hits me. I'm gonna hit him first, hard and often. I'm gonna swarm all over him.'

Honeyghan was so convinced of his destiny that he asked his manager, Mickey Duff, to stake $5,000 of his purse money on him to win, at odds of 5–1. Duff, never loathe to gamble on his own judgement and hunches, bet a similar amount. But apart from those two, and Honeyghan's trainer, Bobby Neill, there was barely a soul in the whole wide world who gave him even a glimmer of a chance. The fight had been billed, optimistically, by Caesars Palace as The Brawl on the Boardwalk. But to the Americans it was disdainfully dismissed as nothing more than a Cakewalk in the Casino for Curry. There wasn't even any admission charge made. The 1,000 or so audience in the casino theatre were all regular patrons at Caesars, all invited on complimentary tickets. They didn't even bother to print a programme. This, after all, was just a routine defence for a great champion, some Limey come over to take a licking.

British boxing was not in good shape at the time. Barry McGuigan had lost his WBA world featherweight title in the desert heat of Las Vegas three months earlier. And Frank Bruno's first assault on the world heavyweight title had ended in a beating by Tim Witherspoon. We desperately needed a new standard-bearer, a champion to raise the morale of a sport that was on its knees. If Honeyghan seemed an unlikely hero, that was a view which owed more to deference to Curry than disrespect for the challenger. Honeyghan, born in the sunshine of Jamaica but raised from the age of nine in the back streets of Bermondsey in South London, had already amassed the British, European and Commonwealth titles.

He was unbeaten in 27 contests – and despite his purely British boxing background he had learned to fight the loose-limbed, mobile American way. 'I taught myself from videos I used to watch for hours in my bedroom. I was the best trainer I ever had. I used to teach my trainers!' he said.

That was the swaggering air of confidence Honeyghan brought to the ring with him. There was also heartening news for the British camp, with rumours that Curry had struggled to make the weight. 'I didn't take a lot of notice of that, but it did make my pre-fight plan all the more important. I intended to jump right on him from the very start, swarm all over him, never give him time to draw breath. If he had been having weight problems, that would make it all the more difficult for him to keep pace with me,' said Honeyghan. 'I was ready to make him feel like he was being attacked by a swarm of angry bees.'

Brave words. And they were more than matched by the almost maniacal assault he launched on the champion from the opening bell. Curry, used to challengers treating him with far more respect, was stunned as he suddenly found himself in the eye of a hurricane. He was used to fighting in his own measured way, dictating the pace and the pattern. But Honeyghan never allowed him to settle even for an instant. The challenger's punches rained in from all angles at such a ferocious speed that Curry found himself being driven backwards in the very first round.

It was a similar frantic story in round two. 'Man, I was so determined that nothing could have stopped me. I was a ragamuffin in that ring – that means I was ready to do anything and everything it took. I wasn't no mere fighter in there. I was a guy ready to win a brawl, a street-fight. I'd trained so hard for this night. I even left the comforts of my own home and lived in the country, living off the land, living like a soldier. That's what I was. A man of war,' recalled Honeyghan.

Curry tried to fight his way back into contention, and in rounds three and four, with the challenger slowing just a little, the American began to land some decent punches of his own. But in round five Honeyghan suddenly charged forward again, forcing Curry into desperate defence. It was a relentless, remorseless assault that continued right through the round. The champion, his face already bruised and swollen by the ravages of Honeyghan's attacking, was a sorry sight as he trudged wearily back to his corner at the end of the round. He came back to sustain another fearful beating in round six. The crowd were shocked into silence, save the tiny British contingent – we were delirious, even if we could barely believe the evidence of our own eyes. By the time the bell came to end the sixth, blood was beginning to trickle from cuts above both the champion's eyes. Curry, his body battered and pained as much as his face, could take no more. He shook his head as he slumped on his stool, signalling his surrender. He had suffered enough from this raging monster.

It was a truly astonishing upset, an unbelievable display of savage, sustained pressure-fighting. Now that it was over, and he had captured the title he always claimed was his destiny, Honeyghan fell full length on the canvas in his uncontrollable excitement. Manager Duff, almost as emotionally overcome as his fighter, leapt into the ring and on top of him, the pair rolling and cuddling on the ring floor, both caught up in the ecstasy of the moment.

Curry was so physically drained by the merciless beating he had suffered that he was taken to hospital. Thankfully, there was no serious damage and, at 1.30 a.m., some five hours after his title had been so brutally plundered from him, he was man enough to convene a hurried press conference in his suite at the hotel. Lying on his bed, the scars on his face vividly betraying his plight, he confessed: 'I did have problems making the weight – but I take nothing away from Lloyd Honeyghan. The man was supercharged.' Honeyghan was basking in the glory of victory in his own, much more modest, room at the hotel. He sat on his bed for the whole night, taking congratulatory telephone calls from England, talking animatedly to anyone who cared to listen. 'I'm the champ. I've beaten the guy they all said was unbeatable. But when you are prepared to take any pain, the way I was, you can beat anybody,' he said.

Honeyghan was to ride a spectacular roller-coaster of triumph and disaster for the next three years, becoming the sometimes brash and bloody-minded but always barnstorming and entertaining flag-bearer for British boxing. He set one remarkable record, knocking out American Gene Hatcher in 40 seconds in Marbella – the fastest world title ending in history. His tempestuous reign finally ended when he was soundly beaten by another American, Marlon Starling, in Las Vegas in 1989. But in defeat Honeyghan showed dignity. He loathed the big-talking Starling 'more than any other guy I've fought'. But he still shook hands with the new champion and congratulated him. 'We're all warriors in that ring, we're all brothers. He's a brave man,' he said. No braver, though, than the ragamuffin man whose night of glory ranks with the greatest in his country's whole sporting history.

Junior Grows Up

Roy Jones Jnr v James Toney

Roy Jones Jnr was born in Pensacola, Florida, on 16 January 1969. He boxed for the USA in the 1988 Olympic Games in Seoul, only to be cruelly robbed of the light middleweight gold medal by a blatant home-town decision for his Korean opponent in the final. He was voted the best boxer of the games and turned professional the following year. He outpointed Bernard Hopkins to win the vacant IBF world middleweight title in 1993 and moved up to capture the IBF super-middleweight title from James Toney 18 months later. He is still unbeaten in his professional career.

ONE ALL-CONSUMING DESIRE drove Roy Jones Jnr to challenge James Toney. 'I knew I was the best middleweight around, but I wanted to prove more than that. I wanted to show the people I was the best fighter, pound for pound, on earth.' It was a seemingly awesome challenge he faced when he stepped into the ring at the MGM casino in Las Vegas on 18 November 1994 to face the IBF world super-middleweight champion. Like Jones, Toney was unbeaten. 'And there's no guy out there can beat me – certainly not this kid Jones,' Toney had trumpeted.

When they first came face to face, Toney's insults were more mocking. 'You better get ready to kiss my ass!' he taunted at the quiet, pensive figure seated next to him. Jones just shrugged it off, refusing to be goaded. 'He thought he was frightening me, but it was exactly the opposite. I could see this guy was just a bully, he was trying to hide his own fear.'

Not many of the 15,000 who crammed into the indoor arena shared Jones's sentiments. After all, Toney was a battle-hardened, proven champion. He had collected an illustrious list of scalps – Michael Nunn, Mike McCallum, Iran Barkley, Prince Charles Williams. And, despite his posturing and his posing, he had always found a way to prevail, in the most testing circumstances. Toney, who had himself moved up from middleweight after finding it increasingly difficult to make the 11 stone 6lbs limit, was unbeaten and unloved. But he was respected as a durable, cussed and awkwardly effective champion.

Jones, by contrast, had precious few victims of note on his 26-fight record. He had come into professional boxing as a hero, on a wave of public sympathy after he was so disgracefully robbed of a gold medal at the 1988 Olympic Games in Seoul. Losing a final he dominated to a Korean had aroused such indignation back home it made him more famous than his team-mates who had triumphed. But his chin was still untested, his open, hands-down style was regarded as too flashy – and he was moving up more than half a stone to the 12-stone division. 'What people didn't know though was that I had also been finding it harder and harder to make the middleweight limit. Those extra pounds were precious to me – they gave me more strength and took nothing away from my speed,' he revealed. 'My training camp for the fight was a pure joy. I was able to eat properly, not starve myself. I felt so good I was ready to burst when I finally got in the ring. By now it had become a bit of a personal thing. I didn't like the way Toney was constantly mouthing at me, telling me what he was going to do to me.'

The casino betting was heavily on Toney winning. But it took just three minutes for Jones to make a total nonsense of all the pre-fight hype. 'I'd really gone to work in the dressing-room, to make sure I was nice and loose from the start,' he said. And that whiplash left hand was crunching into Toney's face from the first bell. Toney, slow and ponderous to protect himself against the machine-gun speed and accuracy of the punches raining in on him, simply had no answer. He was like some plodding grizzly bear trying to corner a snarling leopard. When he came lumbering forward, Jones would deftly slip to one side, leaving him helpless and exposed – and tormenting him with that left hand.

'We knew he would have no answer to my speed and mobility. I'd studied hours of video tapes and I knew he wouldn't be able to live with me, as long as I kept the fight at high-octane level,' said

Jones. If the confused champion was unnerved by the fire raging around him, he was close to humiliation in the third round when Jones, the man whose punching power had been questioned, sent him toppling with a left hook. Toney crumbled against the ropes, which prevented him from the indignity of being put on the seat of his pants. But referee Richard Steele still correctly ruled it a knockdown, even though Toney's pride seemed more wounded than his body.

That pride was to be hurt time and again throughout the remainder of the fight as Jones, beginning to revel in his mastery, produced his own showman's touches. He would feint with the right hand only to send a left thudding into Toney's face, he would shimmy while holding the ropes, put his hands on his hips and thrust his chin forward to goad the increasingly frustrated and forlorn champion . . . What had been billed as a potentially brutal battle became instead a virtuoso performance from a true artist of the ring. Jones was a sorcerer, Toney the victim in his spell. At the end all three judges had the challenger ahead by huge margins. And as Toney slunk away, the new champion said simply: 'God blessed me with a lot of hand speed and foot speed. So I used the gifts He gave me to give myself the edge.'

For those who had doubted and now believed in Jones's genius, the words were rather more fulsome. 'His mobility and manoeuvrability were fantastic – he was like Nuryev in boxing boots!' gasped one. Another labelled him the new Muhammad Ali. It was an interesting observation, because Jones himself is considering moving up eventually to take on the supreme challenge of fighting a heavyweight champion to prove his greatness. 'It can be done. Middleweights used to fight for the heavyweight title quite often in the old days,' he says. 'I know that the heavyweights are much bigger these days. I could never see myself facing a Riddick Bowe or Lennox Lewis for example, because they are just TOO big for me. But a smaller one, if another Evander Holyfield or Michael Moorer comes along – well, that would be interesting.'

It is the new challenge Jones has set himself in his ceaseless quest to become a boxing legend as well as a champion. But that night in Las Vegas he did achieve that first major ambition. He became recognised as pound for pound the greatest fighter in the world.

An Offering for the Gods

Kirkland Laing v Roberto Duran

Kirkland Laing was born in Jamaica on 20 June 1954, but moved to Nottingham with his family while he was still a child. A brilliant amateur boxer, he was National Champion at schools, junior and then senior ABA level. He never fulfilled his enormous potential after turning professional, although he did win the British and European welterweight titles.

FOR THE ONLY TIME in his fighting life, Kirkland Laing felt the cold shiver of fear at he walked gingerly towards the ringside. He was the loneliest man in the world as he stepped through the ropes to be greeted by the kind of merciless, bloodthirsty roar the Roman crowds probably reserved for the original Christians as they were fed to the lions.

It was the night of 4 September 1982, and Laing appeared to be nothing more than a sacrificial offering himself to the crowd jammed into the indoor stadium in Detroit, arguably America's meanest city. Laing had been despatched from England, where his own career had begun to stutter and stumble, to face a legend. Roberto Duran was revered as the hardest, cruellest and most punishing fighter of the day. Not without just cause had he earned his nickname Hands of Stone. But the former world lightweight and welterweight champion from Panama had been beaten by Wilfred Benitez earlier in the year in his challenge for the light middleweight crown. He was rebuilding his reputation – and Laing was seen as no more than fodder to feed his confidence. 'I knew that. I also knew that I had enough skill to stand him on his head. But what I knew most of all was the reputation of this guy. Man, he was brutal, as mean as they come,' says Laing. 'I had nearly 60 pro fights and, while I generally respected the guy in the other corner, I never felt any fear in my life – apart from this time. I knew that this guy wasn't fussy what he hit you with or where he hit you. I'd watched him on video and he used to hit opponents with his forearms and even his elbows. And there were times he hit 'em so low they must have been talking like schoolboys again afterwards! Even watching him on the TV screen used to make my eyes water. And I knew that in front of this crowd he would get away with murder – if I let him.'

Laing, by total contrast, was a man who fought by stealth, cunning – and astonishing india-rubber reflexes. Such was his stunning speed and power of anticipation that, against lesser challengers, he would often stand in front of them, his hands down around his waist, his chin thrust invitingly forward, goading them into charging wildly after him. Then he would clinically pick them off.

If their fighting philosophies were poles apart, they shared a common passion for wild living outside the ring. And in this department few could survive with Laing who, by his own admission, had indulged on binges that would last for days on end. Wine, women and ganja would become his staple diet – and he confesses that his boxing career suffered through his excesses. 'I know it was foolish, man, but that's how it always was for me. I'd just go missing . . .'

Two defeats in his previous three fights, after an earlier run of 18 straight victories, had sounded an ominous warning. He had lost his British welterweight title to Welshman Colin Jones the previous year. He desperately needed at least a creditable performance against Duran to lift those flagging fortunes. But while Laing fretted at the awesome challenge, his manager Mickey Duff, in the ring whispering encouragement to him, was supremely confident. 'I knew that for once, at least, Kirkland was in tip-top physical condition for this fight,' said Duff. 'He'd been out in Detroit training for the past three weeks – and I hadn't let him out of my sight for a second.

'The Americans didn't give him a prayer – I'd taken odds of 7–1 to lay a $5,000 bet on Laing. Because I knew he had the style to frustrate Duran, the way Sugar Ray Leonard had a couple of years earlier. He could drive any opponent mad with the way he used to fight. He was as slippery as an eel.'

The glowering, impatient Duran was to learn the wisdom of those words as he pounded forward at the first bell, determined to sweep this upstart Englishman out of his way early. But there is nothing like the sniff of danger to enliven the senses – and Laing swept easily out of range. It was a pattern that was to continue throughout the ensuing ten rounds. Duran was like an increasingly enraged bull, rushing and boring his way forward with a growing frenzy as the will o' the wisp figure in front of him refused to be cowed.

'Man, he was as wild and as dirty as I ever imagined. His head kept boring in at me – it was as dangerous as his fists!' said Laing. 'But I was floating on air. I was stopping him getting off his big punches inside, I was containing him. And I knew I was winning at long range. He couldn't get a clean shot at me. I'd just dance one way, then the other, never give him a chance to settle his feet. He shook his hands at me a few times, telling me to come forward and fight. But I was quite happy fighting the way I was. All he showed me was that he was getting more and more frustrated.'

Laing kept his composure right to the end, ignoring the jeers and catcalls from a crowd who had grown increasingly restive as Duran failed to deliver the knockout victory they craved. The fans yelled their disapproval at the final bell, too, when Laing was declared the winner by the judges on a majority verdict of 2–1. 'Duran took it like a man. He came over and told me, in his broken English: "You a very smart sonofabitch!" That took some doing, because I could see he was gutted,' said Laing. Within nine months, Duran would add to his legend by becoming a world champion in a third different division, stopping Davey Moore inside eight rounds to plunder the WBA light middleweight title.

But it was now, in the hour of his greatest triumph, that Laing was betrayed by those old demons. His remarkable victory made him one of boxing's hottest properties, with manager Duff inundated with offers from across America. 'I could have got him a world title shot, no question about that,' said Duff. 'But would you believe it, just when he had the world at his feet, he disappeared. And I mean disappeared., He just dropped out of sight, out of the world. Even his own family claimed they didn't know where he was. He could have been dead for all I knew. I never heard a thing from him for six months – then I got a call from the police, after he'd got himself in trouble.'

'You know me . . . I just kinda dropped out for a while,' says Laing, still able to raise a grin at an escapade that cost him a fortune as well as a possible world title. It is, though, a sad epitaph to a career so rich in pedigree, so tarnished by his inability to walk away from the wild side. It left Mickey Duff a loser as well. 'Duran was promoted at the time by Don King, who thought Laing would be an easy fight for him. King was so angry afterwards that he refused to do business with me again for years – it probably cost me a load of money!' said Duff.

Sugar Sweetens the Judges

Sugar Ray Leonard v Marvin Hagler

Ray Leonard was born in Wilmington, South Carolina, on 17 May 1956. He climaxed a wonderful amateur career, in which he lost only five of 150 contests, by winning a gold medal for America in the 1976 Olympic Games in Montreal. He turned professional the following year and captured his first world title, the WBC welterweight crown, in 1979. He went on to unify that title and win the WBA world light middleweight title, before retiring in 1982 after suffering a detached retina. But he returned five years later to score a major upset by defeating Marvin Hagler to win the undisputed world middleweight title. He later added world titles in the super middleweight and light heavyweight divisions, to complete one of the greatest careers in boxing history.

SUGAR RAY LEONARD was the man who had it all. An Olympic gold medal, thrillingly won in Montreal in 1976, then world titles plundered at welterweight and junior middleweight, in epic battles against Wilfred Benitez, Roberto Duran and Thomas Hearns, had already secured his legendary place in boxing's hall of fame. He had earned a staggering $45 million . . . 'Hey, I gotta job just trying to spend the interest!' was his quip. Now he was retired from the ring, but still a hero – and still basking in the public spotlight as ringside analyst for America's Home Box Office satellite television giants. He was also training fighters, starring in TV commercials for several of the country's wealthiest companies, he was honorary chairman for the American Library Association and the National Safety-Belt

Council, and he worked with his attorney and close friend Mike Trainer as part-owners of an up-market restaurant in Maryland, his adopted state.

He also had a detached retina at the back of his left eye which caused him to announce his retirement, on medical advice, in 1982, when he was at the pinnacle of the boxing world, a champion of exquisite artistry, dazzling speed and blistering punching power. In Britain he would never have been allowed to box with such an injury, but American laws are less stringent. In 1984 he attempted a comeback, but struggled to halt journeyman Kevin Howard in nine rounds. 'There's no sense fooling myself – it just isn't there anymore,' he declared. 'That's it.' Now he could enjoy the rest of his life in celebrity status, spending at least a part of the fortune he had earned. But one name, one item of unfinished business had gnawed away inside him since 1982. And it remained obstinately there long after the contest with Howard, right through 1985 and 1986. *Marvin Hagler*! It was a name to strike terror into the ranks of most of those around the middleweight division. Marvelous Marvin was the most destructive, the most feared fighter in the world. He was the undisputed middleweight champion of the world, undefeated in 11 years, a warrior with the blood lust of a modern Genghis Khan – and displaying a similar modicum of mercy inside the ring. It seemed that Hagler's brutality and Leonard's flair were certain to be pitted against each other as Leonard made his way up the divisions in the early '80s. When Leonard announced his retirement, not once but twice, Hagler was equally distraught. He was the blue-collar king of boxing, the idol of the working-classes. He had come up the hard way. Leonard's glorious amateur career had made him so sought after that he was a millionaire before he ever went into the ring as a professional. He had national television exposure from the start, unlike Hagler who had to build up his reputation far away from the glamorous spotlight. For years he had nursed an ambition to give this flashy young pup a good whipping. Now his ambition was to remain unfulfilled. Or was it?

In the autumn of 1986, rumours began that Leonard was working in the gym again. Then he announced to a stunned public that he wanted to return for just one more fight – against Hagler. The match was made for 6 April 1987, fittingly at Caesars Palace in Las Vegas, by now the Mecca of the boxing world. Those who questioned his sanity and feared for his sight were given short shrift. 'I don't want a new career, I just want one fight,' he said. 'And

Hagler's the ultimate challenge, the Everest. This fight was always my dream. I have saved my body for this one. I have saved my mind. I am taking a chance, but I have thought it out carefully.'

So he had, as he now reveals. 'Styles make fights – and I felt I had the style to beat him. I knew I couldn't knock him out because he had shown in the past what a good chin he had. And I was not a hard puncher at the middleweight level. The key was to keep mobile, not to allow him to get set – and also to use my jab to score points.'

The war before the fight, the psychological battle between them, was fascinating. Hagler, normally a kindly and courteous man outside the ring, became obsessive as the date grew nearer. 'I've got the word "hurt" printed in my mind for Ray Leonard. This guy is nothing but an ego trip. He's got everyone wrapped around him, but what happens in the ring? I'll knock him out. I'll prove he is a phoney.' The tirade from the champion suggested he was expending unnecessary energy on his anger at the way that Leonard, the darling of the media, was winning the struggle for hearts and minds.

That rage was ready to explode as the words were finally replaced by action on a gloriously warm Nevada spring night before a huge audience that included most of Hollywood's finest – such was the attraction of a contest labelled 'The Super Fight' by promoter Bob Arum. Hagler, his shaven head adding to his aura of menace, stormed out throwing his big bombs from the start. Leonard was quite content to feel his way cautiously into proceedings – it was only his second fight in five years. But having moved backwards for most of the round, he had the crowd roaring as he suddenly launched his own attack near the end, unleashing punches at windmill speed.

It was a crafty tactic that Leonard was to use over and over again during the dozen rounds. He fought in flashy, flamboyant spurts, no more than 30 seconds at a time in each round. While Hagler would stalk him relentlessly for the remainder of each round, it was those spectacular sorties of the challenger which would raise the crowd to its feet. Leonard played outrageously to the gallery – and to the judges. As the fight wore on and his confidence grew, he was even able to indulge in his own brand of show-boating, teasing and tormenting Hagler. The champion even began to taunt him back towards the end, a dangerous sign that his concentration was wavering. But Hagler was still throwing most of the punches. And while many were cleverly avoided, enough found their target to suggest that, even though he could never quite nail his elusive, darting challenger, he was nonetheless winning the fight. But was he, in the eyes of the three judges? Contests of such contrasting styles are always difficult to score. A judge has ears as well as eyes. He will hear the roar of the crowd, which perhaps can carry as much influence as the more tangible evidence in front of him.

When the final bell sounded and both fighters raised their arms in triumph, each believing himself to be the victor, my own observation from ringside was that both, indeed, had emerged victorious. Hagler's work-rate and the extra power of his punches had earned him a win which, if never comfortable, was nevertheless beyond reasonable doubt. But Leonard was the moral champion. He had confounded those, this hack included, who had questioned the sanity of a man prepared to risk grave injury to his sight in his all-consuming cause. Now he was basking in his glory. And suddenly we realised that a sensation could be about to unfold as the MC announced a split decision. Then the result came. One judge had voted for Hagler, two for Leonard – one of them, Mexican Jose Juan Guerra, by an astonishing ten rounds to two.

Hagler was distraught. 'It's so unfair. It's not right,' he said later. 'I won that fight. He got it because he just fooled people.' The beaten champion had a case. But few wanted to hear it. This was Leonard's greatest moment; he had climbed his Everest. 'That's why I'll always be grateful to Marvin Hagler for fighting me,' he says. 'He gave me rebirth, gave me life again. He made me realise that I could do whatever I wanted to do. Not just by beating him, but by contending with him.' The victory had also brought the lust for glory surging back through his veins. Instead of retiring, he went on to plunder the WBC world super middleweight and light heavyweight titles the following year, becoming champion in five divisions – an astonishing achievement and a fitting epitaph to a wonderful career.

He actually offered Hagler the chance to gain revenge in a return match. 'Mike Trainer made the offer. But there was no reply or response from Hagler. Whether he was bitter or what I don't know, but no response came.' Hagler, indeed, was so emotionally shattered that he never fought again. So what was the force that continued to drive Leonard on? 'I knew I would beat Hagler, because everybody else in the world was convinced I couldn't,' he replies. 'I enjoyed competing at my best – and proving people wrong. I started off in boxing hoping, like all fighters, that it would make me rich and famous. Then it became the love of the sport. I enjoyed doing what I do best in a sport that I was able to totally dominate. At the end of it all, it's down to two words. Fighters fight . . .'

The Right Hand from Hell

Lennox Lewis v Razor Ruddock

Lennox Lewis was born in Stratford, London, on 2 September 1965. He emigrated to Canada with his mother Violet when he was 12 and learned to box in Kitchener, Ontario, his adopted town. He fought for Canada as an amateur and climaxed a wonderful career by winning gold medals in the super heavyweight division in the Commonwealth Games in Edinburgh in 1986 and the Olympic Games in Seoul in 1988. He always retained his British passport and he returned to England to launch his professional career the following year. He became British, European and Commonwealth heavyweight champion before being awarded the WBC title after Riddick Bowe, the champion, had relinquished the title rather than fight him.

HAD HE BEEN AROUND at the time, Lennox Lewis could have restored order to the Tower of Babel. I have never known anyone, certainly not in the frenetic world of boxing, who possessed such a massive, authoritative calming influence as this huge man from the back streets of London's East End who learned his trade in Canada – and, perhaps because of his transatlantic pedigree, returned to Britain to smash his way into sporting legend as our first world heavyweight champion of this century. Not since the gas lamp, Victorian days of Cornishman Bob Fitzsimmons, who reigned from 1897 to 1899, had sport's supreme title ever been held by a man from these shores. Many had tried to break the American monopoly, but all had been found wanting. And the image of the horizontal British heavyweight was a constant source of humour to the Americans – and a gnawing frustration for us. Then, with dramatic speed and the force of a thunderbolt, the answer to our prayers emerged.

Lewis had first captured the attention of the boxing world when he blitzed his way to a gold medal in the super-heavyweight division in the Commonwealth Games in Edinburgh in 1986. Two years later, he became the most sought-after prospect in the sport following his two-round beating of the much vaunted American Riddick Bowe which won him gold again at the Olympic Games in South Korea. His vest bore the maple leaf of Canada on both occasions, so there was no more than a muted interest back in Britain. But Lewis had never forgotten his East End roots. He still retained his British passport and was proud to be a citizen of two countries he loved. Then fate took a hand when he turned professional in 1989 – and, if you'll forgive my indulgence, an interview I conducted with him in Las Vegas led directly to his choosing Britain as his base.

Intrigued by his London connection, I asked him if he had considered moving back to a country where professional boxing was far more in the sporting mainstream than in Canada. He jumped at the suggestion and my colleague, photographer Lawrence Lustig, telephoned Frank Maloney, a hustling young London manager. Maloney found £500,000 financial backing – and within four months Lewis was making his debut against Birmingham journeyman Al Malcolm at the Royal Albert Hall in London. Malcolm was despatched inside two rounds – and that launched Lewis on an all-conquering path that brought him the European title, the British and then the Commonwealth crown within three years and 20 fights.

Britain finally had a hero who really seemed to possess the ammunition to plunder the title which had been beyond us for more than 90 years. By this stage he was rated among the top four heavyweights in the world. Evander Holyfield was the undisputed champion and, with Mike Tyson in jail after being convicted of rape, Lewis, his old Olympic victim Riddick Bowe and the powerful Canadian Donovan 'Razor' Ruddock were the three outstanding challengers. Home Box Office, the giant American television network, organised a box-off among the four. Holyfield would defend his title against Bowe, with the winner guaranteeing a first defence against either Lewis or Ruddock, who signed to meet at London's Earls Court on 31 October – or rather the early hours of the following morning, to accommodate American TV schedules.

Lennox, it seemed, had drawn the short straw in the deal. Ruddock presented a far more formidable barrier than either the brave but small champion Holyfield or Bowe, a man he had already beaten in their amateur days. Ruddock was a couple of years older and more experienced, he had been beaten but certainly not bowed in two ferocious battles with Tyson, he had a left hook of such chilling power that it had become the most feared weapon in boxing – and he had a personal score to settle with Lewis, who had upstaged him in their amateur days, bringing the golden glory to Canada that Ruddock never could.

The pair had sparred often in those days. 'It was more like warfare, until the coaches stopped us,' recalled Lewis. The ill-feeling, from Ruddock in particular, had simmered inside him as the years passed. Yet this was a bitterness which Lewis planned to turn into a weakness. 'When you get two well-matched fighters, it's the man who wins the psychological battle who wins the fight,' he said. 'Razor is a very excitable, volatile kind of guy. Me . . . I can always stay calm, I have a composure which he does not possess. I plan to work on his mind, to make him use up energy he should be saving for the fight.'

Those mind games actually began in Atlantic City, New Jersey's tawdry ocean gambling resort, more than two months before the two fighters stepped into the ring together. Lewis was keeping busy with a warm-up contest against American journeyman Mike Dixon before a star-studded audience including both Ruddock and Bowe. Lennox took the opportunity for a few rounds of useful sparring before halting the outclassed Dixon in the fourth. At the press conference an hour or more later, Ruddock was openly scornful. 'You showed nothing tonight – I feel more certain than ever that I'm gonna knock you out,' he said. and he went on interjecting from the back of the crowded room before Lewis pointed a finger at him and told him, in a mock Jamaican accent, 'Hush your mouth!' Both their families had originated from the sunshine Caribbean island, so this was a severe put-down to Ruddock. Yet, astonishingly, he meekly did as he was told. He shut up. The incident passed unnoticed by most, but it was a classic early demonstration that Lewis had established a mental mastery.

He continued the same tactic when Ruddock arrived in London, accompanied by a huge, noisy entourage of nearly 30 people. Ruddock's cheer-leaders and the assorted crowd of promoters, managers, sportswriters and hustlers thronged his pre-fight hotel headquarters day and night, turning it into a constant circus. Lewis, meanwhile, rested easily at his own hotel hideaway, his whereabouts being the most closely guarded secret in London. When the two were brought together for press conferences, Ruddock invariably sweated profusely – his eyes were wide with a mixture of apprehension and excitement, his adrenalin was flowing already. Lewis, by extreme contrast, was always the coolest, most composed man in the room. If his mind was in turmoil, his impassive face never betrayed even a flicker of emotion, except for the occasional grin when Ruddock would launch himself into one of his tirades. 'I have some nerves before a fight, especially such an important one. But I knew I had trained diligently, my mind was totally focused, I could do no more,' said Lewis. And he must have read my own unsure mind. I thought Lewis could triumph, a view not shared by the majority of the writers covering the fight. But I feared it would be his hardest and most dangerous contest to date. 'I'll tell you this right now – it will be easier than you think,' he assured me. That was enough to put my mind at rest. Lewis, as I have said, has this gift of transferring his own composure and confidence to others.

The huge Earls Court arena was a heaving, rowdy mass of humanity when Lewis was first to make his ring entrance, shortly before one o'clock in the morning. He was accorded an uproarious welcome – the fight had genuinely captured the British imagination. Here, after all the long, barren decades, was a heavyweight truly ready to break the American monopoly. But could he stand up to the brutal power of Ruddock? If there was an almost tangible air of suspense among the packed crowd, though, it certainly did not transmit to Lennox. He had been so relaxed in his dressing-room he had fallen asleep! He had to be gently awakened by his trainer Pepe Correa when it was time to have his hands bandaged.

He remained icily detached in his corner during the preliminaries, in stark contrast to Ruddock who paced about feverishly, his body once again glistening with sweat, his eyes once more betraying the agitated state of his mind. At the first bell he charged towards Lewis, only to be clipped by a sharp left jab which instantly brought him to his senses. From that moment on a tense caution took over the proceedings – until half a minute from the end of the round.

Lewis's brain was working overtime though. He has always been a skilled strategic fighter, as befits a man who includes chess among his passions in life. 'Chess is great training for fighting. Boxing is really chess with muscles, thinking out openings, then striking,' he says. Now his mind was waiting, his eyes were watching intensely, he was priming himself to exploit the opening he knew would present itself. 'When Pepe and I had studied videos of Ruddock, we noticed that every time he threw a jab to the body he would leave his head exposed, just for a fraction of a second, to a right hand over the top. When he was fighting a tall guy like me, that would be a cardinal mistake,' he said. Now, with the first round nearing its close, Lewis suddenly saw the chance. For an instant, as Ruddock threw a rather lazy left jab, the head was open. This was the moment – and Lewis seized it ravenously. A pulverising right hand smashed high into Ruddock's head, landing on the temple. 'It was a few inches too high to be called a perfect punch,' he said later. But it had a catastrophic effect on Ruddock. His legs trembled, he tried in vain to take a step forward and instead he sunk slowly to the canvas. He managed to haul himself up in time to beat the count, but his legs seemed made of rubber, he was quite unable to stand on them with any conviction.

It needed little more than a push to send him down again as Lewis moved in. But the bell came to Ruddock's rescue, enabling him to stagger back to his corner. He was obviously in acute distress, though. 'I looked over at him from my stool and his eyes were wide open, he looked like a man who was not there, mentally speaking. My corner were very excited. They told me to go out there and finish him off while he was still dazed.'

Ruddock, fighting on desperation alone, tried to attack Lewis in the opening seconds of the second round. But his was the frenzy of a drowning man. Lewis, as ever, remained icily calm amidst the bedlam of noise from the screaming audience. He awaited the opening again and, when it came, he smashed another right hand into Ruddock's face, sending him falling to the floor again. This time Ruddock, now reduced to a man surviving on instinct alone, bounced back up at three. Again he tried to force the fight to Lewis, flailing his arms wildly. Lewis simply brushed them off and ended the destruction with a volley of punches to Ruddock's head. As he pitched over for the third time, referee Joe Cortez signalled the end without even bothering to begin a count. Pandemonium broke out as dozens of people invaded the ring and hundreds more laid siege to it. No British heavyweight had ever shown this kind of brutal power before. 'I don't believe anyone in the world could have beaten me on that night,' said Lewis. 'Everything was right – the crowd gave me power, my training gave me strength.'

Boxing being the political game that it is, there was an unsavoury sequel to the fight. Riddick Bowe outpointed Evander Holyfield 13 days later to win the three world title belts – WBC, WBA and IBF. Bowe's camp had already agreed that, if he became champion, Lewis would be his first challenger. But they promptly reneged on their pledge and when the WBC insisted on him defending against Lewis, Bowe, in an act of childish petulance, dumped the belt in a dustbin. Lewis was eventually awarded the title outside the ring. 'It wasn't the way I would have wanted it, but if Bowe refused to fight me there was no other alternative,' he said. 'In any event, I think I proved even to the Americans on that night against Ruddock that I was the best heavyweight in the world.'

Everybody's Darling – At Last

Charlie Magri v Eloncio Mercedes

Charlie Magri was born in Tunisia on 20 July 1956. His family moved to England when he was a child and he was raised in Stepney, in the heart of London's East End. After winning four successive ABA flyweight titles and gaining a bronze medal at the European Championships, he turned professional in 1977. He won the British title in only his third fight and went on to win the European title before capturing the WBC world title towards the end of his career. Magri now runs his own sports shop and also trains boxers.

CHARLIE MAGRI says, 'There are days, very few but golden days in your life when you feel invincible. You feel you could beat the devil himself on those days. Don't ask me to explain it, because I can't. You just feel on a different wavelength, on another planet almost. As if you're just floating along and nothing and nobody can stop you.'

Magri talks from an experience very few of us will ever be privileged to share. For him it helped produce the greatest day of his fighting life, and it brought him a cherished world title he had begun to fear he would never win. Those fears were matched by the thousands who crammed into Wembley Arena on the night of 15 March 1983 when the tailor's cutter from Stepney challenged Eloncio Mercedes for the WBC world flyweight title.

The East End turned up in their multitudes to salute their favourite fighting son. Charlie had been born in Tunisia but raised in their own back streets. He, his four brothers and two sisters, had become as Cockney as jellied eels. He was a fighter in the classic mould of boxing's spiritual heartland . . . tough, aggressive, a boxer when he needed to be, a streetfighter when it came to a brawl and, most importantly of all, blessed with the punching power of a mule.

Magri had reigned supreme in the amateur ranks, winning the ABA title four years in a row. He reached the semi-finals of the European Championships and was hailed as a future world champion when he turned professional in 1977. He had launched his paid career with hurricane force, plundering the British title in only his third fight – still a record – and adding the European crown after only nine more fights. In barely two years he was the number one contender for both the WBC and WBA titles – the only two world governing bodies in those less political days. It seemed only a matter of time before the ultimate prize would be his. So he just waited – and waited. He continued to draw massive crowds to Wembley and the Royal Albert Hall as he smashed his way past all-comers. But that world title kept slipping elusively from his grasp.

'I got so frustrated, so fed up, that I started losing my edge. I got mentally jaded, stale,' he says. 'I was a big occasion fighter, a mood fighter. I needed the challenge to bring the best out of me. But it wasn't happening. The way things were going I knew I was in danger of blowing it all.' That's what sadly seemed to have happened when he was dramatically knocked down and stopped inside half a dozen rounds of mayhem by a Mexican banger named Juan Diaz at the tail-end of 1981. He was beaten again six months later. Now it appeared that a career so rich in promise was to end without fulfilment.

'By that stage I really began to believe that the world title was just a fading dream,' says Magri. 'I know to this day that I would have won both those fights had I been anywhere near my best. But that's what happens to a fighter when he's kept dangling on a string. This game is 90 per cent a mental one. If two fully fit, evenly matched boys get into a ring together, it's the one with the greater desire who will win. I just didn't have the desire on those nights – and I paid the price for it.'

But he pulled his shattered mind together to retain his European crown and then to avenge that second defeat by Jose Torres, outgaming the Mexican to win on points. Promoter Mickey Duff, perhaps sensing that time was beginning to run out for Magri, then finally won him the chance he craved when he persuaded Mercedes to come to London to defend his crown. The champion, from the

Dominican Republic, had won the title only four months earlier, but he had defeated a fine champion, Mexican Freddie Castilo, to do so and that had made him a well-respected figure. Hence the mood of apprehension that hung heavily over Magri's followers as they awaited their hero's entrance. They were here because they owed it to him – but they feared a wake.

'I knew a lot of people had already written me off. I could even understand why they did so,' says Magri. 'But I knew, I just KNEW from the time I woke up that morning that the title was mine. When you want something as badly as I did, you just get a total tunnel vision. You don't see anything or hear anything. All you see, in your mind, is that guy you're going to have to beat up. There's no compassion, but there's no hatred either. Just a cold, ruthless determination.'

It took just seconds for that pent-up fury to explode on Mercedes. From the first bell, Magri was a man inspired. The ferocity of his assault had the champion going backwards, defending desperately to try and stem the tide. But Charlie would not be denied. This was his night of destiny and nothing would stop him.

Mercedes, certainly not lacking when it came to courage, began to fight back with everything he could muster. He hit his challenger with powerful punches of his own, causing blood to flow from a cut on Magri's lip. But that served only to intensify Magri's desire. As the rounds went by and the war of attrition grew ever more gruelling, the champion's own face began to suffer the effects of ceaseless bombardment. He managed to stay on his feet when lesser men would have wilted. But Magri was already building a substantial lead, the champion growing increasingly weary. Blood eventually began to trickle from a vicious cut over his eye. By the seventh round that trickle had become a torrent, leaving Mercedes almost blind. Even a man of his bravery could not carry on under such a crippling handicap and the contest was mercifully stopped. The boxing world had a new champion – and how those East Enders celebrated!

A local pub had been granted a late-night extension and it seemed that half of London was jam-packed inside to acclaim the new king when he arrived. Charlie had always been their darling – now they gave him an uproarious coronation. But Magri didn't stay there too long. He was bruised, sore, exhausted – and starving. 'My wife Jackie and myself and a couple of close friends just slipped out quietly and went round the corner to the Venus Steak House in Bethnal Green Road for something to eat,' he said. 'I couldn't have a steak because my mouth was so sore and swollen I couldn't have chewed anything. So I had to settle for chicken. And even then they had to take all the skin off it so I could swallow it without having to chew it first!'

Charlie's reign did not last long. In truth he was past his brilliant best by this time and he surrendered the crown to Philippino Frank Cedeno in his first defence six months later. 'I think I would have been champion for years if I had been given the chance earlier,' he sighs. 'I would maybe have made a lot more money as well. But at least now, for the rest of my life, I'll always be known as a former world champion. Somebody who's really been there. And, as I said before, on that night I could have licked them all.'

The Bounce of the Yo-yo Man

Dave McAuley v Fidel Bassa

Dave McAuley, born in Larne on 15 June 1961, became Ireland's most successful boxer in a career that included nine world title fights – six of which he won. He collected the British flyweight title in 1986 knocking out Joe Kelly in Glasgow, then won the IBF world title three years later, outpointing Duke McKenzie in London. He retained that title on five occasions – a record at the time for a British fighter. Now retired, McAuley owns a hotel on the outskirts of his home town.

NOT FOR NOTHING will Dave McAuley be remembered as boxing's india-rubber man. Sixteen times in his nine world title fights he was knocked down. Fifteen times he bounced up again. And more often than not, his own powerful punching would send his opponent crashing to the canvas as well. 'Nobody could ever deny that my fights were exciting,' he says with massive understatement.

Yet McAuley, who hails from the Northern Ireland seaside town of Larne, some 20 miles from the bustle of the capital, Belfast, always felt he was a man fated to walk in the shadow of his illustrious countryman Barry McGuigan. 'If I had a problem in my career, it was that I came too close behind Barry,' he says. 'I was always compared with him. And that made it tough for me. We were good pals, but I just wanted to be known for myself.'

Indeed, it was barely ten months since McGuigan had lost his world title when McAuley was given his first big chance. The date was 25 April 1987, the Kings Hall, Belfast, the venue. Fidel Bassa, the Colombian holder of the WBA world flyweight title, was his opponent. Bassa had created a sensation the previous year by outpointing the almost invincible Panamanian Hilario Zapata, veteran of 18 world title fights, to plunder the crown. McAuley had gone to Glasgow six months earlier to capture the British title with a ninth-round stoppage of Joe Kelly, but while he was still unbeaten he had never fought in such exalted company before.

Boxing was still a part-time occupation for McAuley, who continued to work as a chef in his family's restaurant in his home town. 'I always wanted to keep the job going because I never had all that much confidence in my boxing ability,' he admits. 'To be honest, the main thought on my mind as I approached that fight was that there would be an awful lot of Irishmen there supporting me – and I didn't want to let them down by being knocked out in the first round!'

That fear came close to humiliating reality as McAuley was punched to the canvas almost before he had time to raise his hands in self-defence. 'There I was, sat on my arse, put there by his right hand. The crowd had suddenly hushed. I could almost hear the silence,' he said. 'Luckily, I still had control of my mind. I just thought to myself: "I can't stay down here. I couldn't live with all these people if I let them down like that." So I climbed up and managed to survive the round. In fact it was probably the best thing that could have happened to me. I'm a slow starter at the best of times but I felt I was in a bit of a dream at the start.

'It was far and away the biggest occasion of my life and I think I was a bit overawed by it all. But that punch woke me up, got me back to reality. It guess it must be the fighting Irishman inside me, but Bassa made me mad. I just wanted to get to him, pay him back.' He did, too – with interest – in what became an unforgettable battle, a contest of such bruising ferocity and almost unbearable drama that even the thousands thronging the Kings Hall were drained of emotion at the end.

McAuley came back with manic force after his stunning early reversal. So much so that Bassa, who must have expected an early and easy pay-day, suddenly found himself caught up in an Irish whirlwind. He was sent tumbling to the floor in the third round, then in the seventh. But he showed a champion's courage of his own to climb up both times, then carry the battle to McAuley, rocking the challenger with his own big punches.

As the pace grew ever more frenzied, the punishment ever more severe, that crowd, so hushed in the first round, were screaming now as they sensed a sensation, a new king about to be crowned. Then, in the ninth round, it seemed that McAuley really was about to realise his improbable dream. 'I saw an opening and threw a peach of a left hook. It caught him perfect – and down he went,' he said. 'He got up, but I knew he was badly hurt this time, so I went for the finish. I hit him with a flurry of punches and down he went again. Again he managed to scramble on to his feet, but he was rubber-legged by now. And I knew the three-knockdown rule was in force. I only had to put him down once more in the round and the title was mine. I went wild for the kill. But, you have to give him credit, he ducked and dived, grabbed on to me and wouldn't let go. And he survived until the bell.'

That ferocious assault had taken as much from McAuley as it did from the champion. Sheer exhaustion had set into both men. For three more rounds they pummelled each other, draining their last reservoirs of strength. 'I think we were both fighting on memory by that time,' recalled McAuley. 'When the bell went for the end of the twelfth round I could barely raise the energy to crawl back over to my stool. But there were sill three rounds to go. This was the last 15-round world title fight staged in Britain – and that was the irony. I was ahead on the judges' scorecards after 12 rounds, I would have won the title had the fight been a few months later.'

But right now, with three rounds, nine minutes, still remaining, he had nothing left to offer. 'He hit me in the 13th round and down I went. It wasn't that hard a punch but once I was on the floor I just couldn't get back on my feet again. I didn't have the strength to climb up. I was so shattered I couldn't even feel disappointment as the fight was stopped. Just sheer exhaustion. He must have felt just the same. But good luck to him, he showed himself a great champion by the way he came back.'

So memorable was the fight that it was voted by an American boxing magazine as the Flyweight Fight of the '80s and the third best fight of the decade in all divisions. Their rematch a year later was, perhaps understandably, an anti-climax as Bassa easily outpointed a challenger who had been suffering from flu. But McAuley was to realise his world ambitions when he outpointed Duke McKenzie in London in 1989 to win the IBF version.

'I only took the fight for the money. I planned to retire after the second Bassa fight because I felt I would never become a world champion. But the money from the McKenzie fight was going to help set me up in business,' he said. Instead, McAuley went on to successfully defend the title five times, making him Britain's most enduring world champion, before finally losing a disputed points decision to another Colombian, Rudolfo Blanco, in Bilbao in 1992.

'That fight broke my heart, because I knew inside me that I had won. But all in all, I have only great memories of world title fights,' he said. 'Yet, for all the title fights I won, that first fight with Bassa has to be the greatest one I was ever involved in. I still get a little shudder just thinking about it.'

Geordie's Kingdom

Glenn McCrory v Patrick Lumumba

*Glenn McCrory was born in Stanley, Co Durham, on 23 September
1964. A Junior ABA champion, he launched his professional career as a
heavyweight at the age of 19. Despite his 6ft 4ins height, he lacked the
bulk to succeed in the division and moved down to the newly created
cruiserweight division in 1987. He became Commonwealth and then
British champion before outpointing Kenyan-born Patrick Lumumba to
win the vacant IBF world title in 1989. Surprisingly for an area rich in
boxing folklore, he was the first man from the North-east of England to
capture a world title. McCrory is now the highly respected ringside
expert for Sky Sport.*

GEORDIELAND was in mourning in the early summer of 1989.
The shipyards and the coalmines were in decline and, even more
traumatically, Newcastle United and Sunderland football clubs had
both been relegated. The area, already the most depressed in
England, desperately needed a hero, a man to help restore their
morale, lift their battered self-confidence. When Glenn McCrory
stepped in to answer the crisis, he had his own personal motivating
force as well. The Louisa Leisure Centre in his home town, Stanley,
where he was to challenge American-based Kenyan Patrick
Lumumba for the vacant IBF cruiserweight title, was just a few
doors away from the local dole office. 'I'd been inside there to sign
on often enough over the past few years to get a shiver every time I
went past. I never wanted to go back in again. But I knew that's
where I would end up if I lost this fight,' recalled McCrory,

thankfully able to smile ruefully nowadays at the memories. It was a poignant human aside to an event, an occasion as improbable as any even boxing could conjure. The North-east of England, for all its rich heritage of fighting men, had never spawned a world champion. Even more remarkably, the area had never even staged a world title fight before.

'When Lumumba was finally enticed to come here, I was thrilled. I expected the fight to take place at Newcastle or Sunderland. But when the local council at Stanley decided they would put everything into bringing it to my home town it was just unbelievable, fantastic,' said McCrory. 'Imagine it – a world title fight in Stanley. Most people in Britain, never mind the rest of the world, had never even heard of the place. Now it was going to be on the map like never before.' The Labour council joined forces with local businessmen to make the dream a reality. A local brewery gave him a car to use, while another firm laid on a minibus for his training team. And local builders even laid a road to give him access to his training camp, based in a nearby hotel where all the meals were on the house!

McCrory, although still only 24 at this time, had already endured a roller-coaster career. Because he was 6ft 4ins tall, he seemed a natural heavyweight when he turned professional at just 19. 'The trouble was that my natural weight was only around 14 stone. I had to bulk up a stone which was really no more than flab,' he recalled. 'My first manager, Doug Bidwell, always seemed more interested in my eating than my training! I started off all right, winning my first 13 fights. But the truth was I couldn't punch my weight. When the quality of the opposition was stepped up I lost four in a row. I was out of my depth. And my training had sometimes been no more than farcical. I remember training for one fight with my wife being my only sparring partner. We used to train in the kitchen, with her wearing the glove-pads!'

McCrory moved from Bidwell to an American named Beau Williford, who spotted instantly that he was no heavyweight, but would be perfectly suited to the 13stone 8lb cruiserweight division. Williford took McCrory across the Atlantic to resurrect his career with a couple of easy contests to rebuild his shattered confidence. The pair then returned to England, where within a year McCrory captured the Commonwealth title, then the British one. He went back to America to score a couple more victories to put himself in line for a world title shot. His chance came when Evander Holyfield, the dynamic, undisputed champion, relinquished his titles to move up to the heavyweight division.

McCrory was ranked by all three bodies, but he decided to bid for the IBF title against Lumumba, an opponent of genuine pedigree, having formerly been the world amateur champion. 'On pure skill and talent he was better than me, but I was backing my determination. All the more so when it worked out I was going to fight in front of my own people,' he said. But not even Glenn anticipated the extent to which the fight would capture the public's imagination.

The sports centre would normally accommodate only about 1,500 spectators. 'But for this occasion, they took off the doors, changed all the regulations, made space where none existed – and they crammed more than 2,000 in the place!' said McCrory. 'And they could have sold the place five times over. There were hundreds just milling around the centre all day, just enjoying the occasion. There were still hundreds lining the way when I went in. It was a fantastic feeling, having all these people, your own folk, rooting for you like that. I was so emotionally charged up it felt like I was floating through it all. And when I came into the ring, I was greeted by a roar louder than anything I've ever heard before – or since. I've never heard a noise like it. The intensity was overwhelming. And I tell you this – those fans helped to instil into me a feeling of invincibility that night. This was one night in my life when I knew I was going to win. It may sound silly, but there was not one man on earth who could have beaten me – not even Mike Tyson.'

McCrory's plan was to keep the crowd at fever pitch by beginning the fight at a frantic pace, to unnerve still further an opponent who must already have been awestruck by the tumult around him. It almost brought him a sensational knockout victory inside the first minute. 'I hit him with a big left hook. He buckled and grabbed my legs, to stop himself tumbling over,' said McCrory. 'It was a dream start and I kept the pressure on him at full blast for the first four rounds.

'But then, in round five, he started showing some brilliant moves of his own. I remember thinking to myself as he slipped my punches and caught me with a few of his own, "Oh, my God, can this guy fight!" And then he threw a big right hand which caught me flush on the ear – and perforated my eardrum. It was agony. But I just had to grit my teeth and carry on taking the fight to him.' McCrory continued to press relentlessly forward right through the dozen rounds. 'When I was feeling desperately tired in round 11 the crowd started banging the metal seats, making the noise even louder than it had been. That gave me the little extra spur I needed,' he said. He battered the hapless Lumumba unmercifully through the last round to send the crowd into hysteria as he was awarded a unanimous verdict.

'In my whole life I've never known anything like the ecstasy of that moment when the referee holds up your hand and the MC announces you are the world champion. I'd done it, I'd accomplished what every fighter dreams of. But that elation, strangely, is only a fleeting thing. Within an hour or so I couldn't help having this feeling of anti-climax. Mind, even by the time I got to bed, which was several hours later, I still wouldn't take the world title belt off. I'd heard fighters say before that they went to bed with their belt still on and I'd laughed. But I have to admit that I slept with the belt still around my waist!'

McCrory admits that the rest of his boxing career never again reached the pinnacle of that famous and unforgettable night. Increasingly struggling with weight problems, he lost the title within a year and after a couple of brief, fresh excursions he finally called it a day. 'I only earned about £12,000 for the fight, because most of the purse was spent on luring Lumumba over here. And I had to pay two managers out of that – Beau Williford and George Bidwell,' he said. But it did reap a welcome and well-deserved harvest. Sky Television executives were impressed by his demeanour and his articulate manner. He was invited to join them when the satellite company branched into boxing. He has become a splendidly knowledgeable partner to their renowned commentator Ian Darke.

'We're good pals as well as working together. But there's one commentary of Ian's that I have a copy of at home that I cannot bear to listen to,' says McCrory. 'He was the BBC radio commentator at ringside that night in Stanley. He still says it was one of the most thrilling nights of his life and the commentary is so powerful and moving to me that I just get a lump in my throat when I hear it. I get so filled up I have to leave the room before I start crying.'

A Cyclone Hits West London

Barry McGuigan v Eusebio Pedroza

Barry McGuigan was born in Clones, Co Monaghan, in the Republic of Ireland, on 28 February 1961. He was only 17 years old when he won a gold medal in the 1978 Commonwealth Games in Edmonton, Canada. After turning professional he took out British citizenship to enable him to win the British featherweight title. He then captured the European title, before defeating Panamanian Eusebio Pedroza to win the WBA world title in 1985.

SATURDAY, 8 JUNE 1985 . . . and a corner of West London has become the pumping, pulsating heart of Ireland! More than 26,000 people have crossed the Irish Sea, by boat and plane, to be at Loftus Road, home of Queens Park Rangers Football Club, for a night destined to rank with the greatest in the sporting history of their troubled country. The cause of all their noisy expectations is a slip of a boy, just nine stone wet through, who has united a society torn apart by sectarian violence like no priest or politician ever could. Barry McGuigan, the greatest fighting machine the Emerald Isle ever spawned, is here to challenge for the WBA world featherweight championship – and to cement his place in history.

Eusebio Pedroza, the champion from Panama, has reigned supreme for an astonishing 19 defences. In the eyes of many shrewd judges he is invincible, a calculating, cold-eyed Grand Master of the ring, blessed with a deadly combination of stealth and power. It is a classic confrontation, the skill and experience of the wily old campaigner against the dynamic thrust of the young challenger. For

McGuigan, however, it is far more than a boxing summit. This is his holy war, a personal pilgrimage to bring at least a shaft of light to the despair that pervaded the bomb-ravaged streets of Belfast, the city he loved, the city which had adopted him as its favourite fighting son.

'At least I knew that when I was fighting those streets were safe. For once all the people, Catholic and Protestant, were united in a common cause,' recalled McGuigan. Safe? Those streets were deserted! Any Irishman not privileged to be among the noisy, jostling and highly partisan audience at ringside was at home or in a public bar, eyes glued to the television screen – part of an incredible 20 million congregation, the length and breadth of Britain, who were tuned in for a contest which had gripped the imagination of the whole nation. For Barry had captured the hearts and minds of Britain like no fighter before him. He was the devout Catholic from Clones, a tiny township straddling the border, just on the Republic side of the island, who showed his own distaste for religious bigotry by marrying his childhood sweetheart, Sandra Meehan, a Protestant.

He took out British citizenship to enable him to fight for – and to win – the domestic title. Then he did his best to bridge the great divide in Northern Ireland. 'We decided that I should follow a flag of peace into the ring, to avoid a situation where one side would claim I was selling out to the other,' he said. 'I just wanted to try to help the people understand that no matter what church they went to, they were all the same – all human beings.' The people loved him for that. That's why Catholics and Protestants mingled happily and peacefully at Loftus Road on that balmy summer night. Yer Man belonged to them both.

What they did not know was that McGuigan's handlers had spent several days in a vain and increasingly frantic search for that flag of peace! 'It was one we had been told was used by the United Nations – white doves on a blue background.' The team trekked all over London without success. Then one was finally spotted – flying proudly outside the Holiday Inn in West London, the very hotel in which they were encamped.

That solved one problem, but there was tension and apprehension in the warm night air as well. Pedroza, they all knew, was a truly formidable fighting force. Would he carry too much savvy and know-how for their indomitable hero? Would the Clones Cyclone be simply blown away? Pedroza had already attempted to rile the pale young challenger when they were brought together for a press conference the day before the fight, claiming McGuigan was a 'scared man'. 'Scared? He couldn't have been more wrong. It was exactly the opposite. I was so excited, so thrilled, I couldn't even sleep for more than a couple of hours the night before. I knew I was facing a great champion, I knew I would have to put on the fight of my life – but that was the way I wanted to win the world title. In a nutshell, I wanted to beat the best.'

There were supporters who were concerned about McGuigan fighting away from his beloved Kings Hall, the Belfast arena he had turned into his own kingdom with a succession of spectacular victories to earn his world title chance. But Barry was not bothered. He had travelled 5,000 miles, to Edmonton, Canada, to win the Commonwealth Games gold medal as a tiny 17-year-old waif back in 1978 – the triumph which had propelled him towards stardom even before he laced his first glove as a professional. 'I knew that my fans would be out in force in London. As long as I had their support, it didn't matter where the fight took place,' he said.

McGuigan had kept one secret locked away from all the world, bar a trusted few people around him. He had been suffering from a heavy cold for most of the week leading up to the big night. 'I didn't want people to know, because I didn't want anything to risk my big chance,' he said. That cold, though, was replaced by a fever as he bounded his way to the ring, to an uproarious welcome. 'That was brought on by all the excitement,' he said. There was no question that his adrenalin was overflowing as he danced and flexed his body in his corner of the ring during the preliminaries. And those high emotions spilled into tears as his father, Pat, who sadly died a few years later, led the audience in a frenzied rendition of 'Danny Boy', Barry's fighting anthem. Pat was a well-known singer throughout Ireland – he once represented them in the Eurovision Song Contest, finishing a creditable third. 'I was on such a high – I was at fever pitch – that I barely had control of my feelings,' said Barry.

Pedroza's impassive, poker face was a vivid contrast. The champion had been momentarily disconcerted when he stepped into the ring to be greeted by a 'leprechaun', a midget dressed all in green, who had been hiding underneath the floorboards. Even Pedroza looked startled as the apparition tumbled and somersaulted around him, scattering glitter dust in his wake. Someone in McGuigan's camp had watched a video of one of Pedroza's previous defences, against a challenger noted for his superstition. Before the fight began, a 'witch doctor' had climbed into the ring and cast a spell on the opponent – who promptly froze with fear! But Pedroza was too worldly wise to be distracted for more than a few seconds. The crafty ploy did not work, as Barry ruefully remembers. 'When that first bell went, I was so wound up I just tore across the ring at him, hell for leather. And he must have been the coolest man in the place. He just picked me off with his jab. I was swinging punches like a madman – and missing with just about all of them.'

So first blood, or at least the opening round, went to the iceman, the cucumber-cool champion. But it was to prove the only time in the fight he was ahead. Those three frenetic minutes had taken the wildness out of McGuigan. 'I was a different fighter by round two, much calmer and more composed,' he said. 'I guess I needed to just get through that first round to take the excitement out of my system. Now I was able to think rationally, like a fighter, to concentrate on the job ahead rather than have my mind dazzled by the bigness of the occasion.

'Straight from the start of the second round I was beginning to find my range, getting my combinations going. And I knew I was starting to hurt him already. His face gave nothing away, but I just sensed I was getting to him.' So began a gruelling, pulsating war of attrition, with the 24-year-old challenger almost invariably that little bit stronger, that little bit sharper – and carrying that little bit more devil to drive him relentlessly on. 'I knew the fight was going my way in the third round, when he hit me with his hardest punches – and I didn't flinch. That told me he couldn't knock me out. It was a great comfort to know that,' recalled McGuigan.

Barry did still have one lingering fear lurking inside him, however. Unknown to the masses who were screaming him on as they watched him swarm over Pedroza – and certainly unknown to the champion – his left arm was beginning to cause him severe pain. 'I damaged a ligament in the elbow five days earlier – at one stage I feared the fight would be called off,' he said. 'I had treatment every day, which meant I was able to carry on. What with the cold as well, it had been a right old build-up! But the left hand was really beginning to jar every time I threw a punch from about the fourth round on. I just had to grit my teeth, make sure he couldn't see I was in any trouble.'

The distress did not prevent him from continuing his relentless, unstoppable assault on the champion. This was his night of glory and nothing was going to spoil it for him. Pedroza summoned every ploy he had ever learned in an increasingly desperate attempt to keep the challenger at bay. But he finally buckled in the seventh round, crashing to the floor from a swinging right cross. The crowd went wild, sensing the kill. If his crown was slipping, though, the 32-year-old Panamanian was grimly determined it would take every last gasp of McGuigan's breath to plunder it from him. He climbed unsteadily up at the count of six and somehow managed to clutch, grab and frustrate McGuigan for the final minute of a round as memorable for the champion's courage as the challenger's irresistible desire. 'Give him credit for that. But that was the moment when I knew the fight was mine, that only doing something absolutely stupid would stop me from winning that title,' said McGuigan. 'I had to keep my head, that was the crucial thing. I remembered the best bit of boxing advice I've ever been given, from a great former champion, Ken Buchanan. "Keep the ice bucket on," he told me. In other words, never let your heart run away with your head. Keep thinking, keep concentrating at all times. That's what I had to remember for the rest of the fight.'

He acted brilliantly on Buchanan's advice, continuing to fight at such a high-octane level that Pedroza could never enjoy the luxury of time to launch his own assault. 'The later rounds were almost like being in a dream. I just seemed to float through them,' he said. 'I remember the incessant roar from the crowd, then my corner getting very excited at the end of the 14th round. "Just three more minutes and it's yours!" they were yelling. The noise was getting louder and louder all the time through that last round. Then the final bell – and I was a little bit disappointed I hadn't knocked him out or stopped him.

'Waiting for the verdict seemed like forever. I knew I'd won, but you always have that nagging doubt that judges may have seen it differently to you.' When the announcement finally came, McGuigan had won by a landslide on the cards of all three judges. Pandemonium broke out both inside and around the ring as the celebrations began. But as his hand was raised, amid all the ecstasy around him, suddenly the tears flowed again from the new champion. 'It was right there and then that the memory of Young Ali came flooding back to me,' he said. Ali was an African fighter who had died tragically after a bruising battle with McGuigan a few years previously. Such was Barry's bitter remorse at the time that he actually stopped training for six months and was ready to retire from the sport he loved. 'In the end I came back. Just walking away from boxing would have proved nothing. At least this way I always knew that if I ever did win a world title I could dedicate it to his memory,' he said. McGuigan has also sent regular money-orders to Ali's widow and family, an act he has always been reluctant to talk about publicly.

It was nearly an hour before he could safely leave the ring without being mobbed. He was whisked back to his hotel, where hundreds of jubilant supporters joined the party that lasted until dawn. But of the new champion there was no sign. Barry, his wife Sandra and their young son Blaine were all tucked up in bed. Their celebration? A bagful of McDonald's burgers, brought in from a local all-night burger bar! 'They were always our special after-fight treat,' he grinned.

McGuigan was to enjoy two more memorable nights, defending his title in Belfast and then in Dublin, before being dethroned by Steve Cruz in the furnace heat of Las Vegas the following summer. His career, spectacular as it was, never quite achieved its full potential. But that wondrous night in West London remains enduringly one of British sport's great occasions.

Fear is a Deadly Weapon

Duke McKenzie v Gaby Canizales

Duke McKenzie was born in Croydon, South London, on 5 May 1963. He turned professional at the age of 19 and, in a distinguished career, became the first British fighter to win world titles in three divisions, the IBF flyweight title, the WBO bantamweight title and then the WBO junior featherweight title. He then fought for the WBO featherweight title, but was knocked out by Steve Robinson. He also won the British and European flyweight crowns.

FEAR IS THE GREATEST motivating force in boxing. It was cold fear which haunted Duke McKenzie constantly for weeks before he challenged Texan Gaby Canizales for the WBO world bantamweight title at the Elephant and Castle Leisure Centre, London, on 30 June 1991. 'Not a day went by in the build-up to that fight when I wasn't filled with terror,' he admits. 'I couldn't sleep at nights either for thinking about him. I knew he was an explosive puncher, he was going to hit me harder than I had ever been hit before. I knew that this was a fight in which I could get hurt – badly hurt. I also knew that defeat would leave my career going up a blind alley. I would be finished as a major force.'

All fighters live with fear – not of being hurt physically but of being embarrassed, humiliated, of being knocked out, of losing their pride. But this time the raw, stomach-churning emotion was something the highly likeable McKenzie had never suffered before – or has since. 'I think it started from the first time I ever thought about fighting Canizales,' he said. 'I went to my manager and promoter, Mickey Duff, and put the idea to him – and he told me I must be crazy to even think about it! But he made some telephone calls, then the offer to persuade Canizales to come to London to defend the title against me. That's when I really began to realise what I was taking on. Everybody, even the people I regard as my closest friends, were all adamant that I shouldn't take the fight. They all feared for me. And when you keep hearing talk like that, it's bound to get through to you in the end.'

The apprehension was understandable. Canizales was the older of two famed fighting brothers from Laredo – brother Orlando was the reigning IBF bantamweight champion. While Orlando was blessed with superb skills, Gaby was the streetfighter, the man with the explosive punching power which had demolished the highly capable Colombian Miguel Lora inside two rounds when he plundered the title just three months previously. He had also reigned as WBA champion and was a grizzled veteran of 45 fights – all bar nine of which he had won inside the distance.

What made his power even more disturbing to McKenzie's friends was that Duke had spent the vast majority of his nine-year professional career as a flyweight – a half stone lighter than the man he was now due to face. Only after he lost his IBF world flyweight crown to Ireland's Dave McAuley did he move up. As a bantam, he had already been outpointed by Frenchman Thierry Jacob in Calais in his bid to win the European title. Now he was taking on the biggest puncher in the division. And the closer the showdown loomed, the more the cold sweats increased. 'By the afternoon of the fight, I was in a terrible state. So bad that I was chucking it up. Yes, I was physically sick. But that's when Dudley [his brother, now tragically dead] came to my rescue. He was always my biggest supporter. Now he started talking to me, telling me I had the skill and the talent to make this guy look a mug.

'Right to the time I was in the dressing-room he kept drilling the same message: just be positive, don't let him overawe you, stamp your authority on the fight from the start. And that's just what I did. By the time I got into the ring I was a different person. I used all that fear – and all his encouragement – to build up a momentum that was going to carry me through the whole ordeal. Honestly, by the first bell I was so wound up, yet so much in control of myself, I felt invincible. It was like I was floating along. The place was packed and I heard the roars for me all the way up to the ring. That made me even more determined – I couldn't let all these people down as they had paid to support me even though they didn't expect me to win.'

McKenzie went on to produce one the most flawless performances any British fighter has ever displayed in winning a world title. 'I got my jab working, my feet moving, right from the first bell,' he recalled. 'He was trying to set himself up for a big attack, but I was in his face and out again before he had time to blink. I felt so fit and so strong. That seven pound difference might not seem much, but for little guys like me it means a different world. I had been struggling to make the flyweight limit for quite a time before I lost that title. Now I was able to eat properly in my build-up. The extra pounds certainly didn't slow me up – and they made me so much more durable. I hadn't done myself justice against Jacob because I'd been out of the ring for 11 months before I fought him. But I'd had a couple of wins since then to build up my confidence, get me used to the weight. And by now I was enjoying the fruits of it all.'

For round after relentless round, McKenzie peppered the champion's face with his jab, never giving Canizales the opportunity to land his own big punches. It was a purist's delight, a victory for sheer skill over brute force. 'I could see he was getting more and more puzzled, then apprehensive. He must have sensed his title was slipping away,' said McKenzie. 'But I didn't relax, even for one second. I dare not. One big punch could have changed everything – and I knew that. I wasn't going to give up everything I had gained now.'

Canizales rallied bravely in the closing rounds, without ever looking capable of stopping the whirlwind that had enveloped him. By the end, victory for McKenzie – a result precious few had dreamed could happen – had become a formality. All three judges had him nine rounds or more ahead. The crowd erupted at the verdict. But, for the hero, there was only a sudden emptiness inside. 'It's a funny thing, but once a fight is over your adrenalin stops flowing, you just become desperately tired, win or lose. You want to get away from everything, find somewhere quiet to flop down.'

McKenzie's roller-coaster career was to bring heartache when he lost the title in a stunning first-round knockout by Puerto Rican Rafael Del Valle eight months later. 'I don't like excuses, but I had been ill before that fight, suffering from flu. I didn't want to fight, but I was persuaded to,' he says. But five months after that he bounced back with another astonishing victory, moving up to junior featherweight to plunder the WBO world title from American Jesse Benavides. That created his niche in history as the first, and thus far the only, British fighter to win world titles in three divisions.

He challenged for an incredible fourth in 1994, producing determined resistance before being knocked out by a perfect body punch by WBO world featherweight champion Steve Robinson. But even had he triumphed in Cardiff that night, his victory over Canizales would still have held pride of place in his memory. 'I have the fight on video and I watch it frequently – especially when I feel a bit down,' he said. 'It was the night when I conquered fear, made it work for me. I can think of no better advice to pass on to any young fighter.'

Springheeled Supermac

Colin McMillan v Maurizio Stecca

Colin McMillan was born in Barking, Essex, on 12 February 1966. He did not launch his professional career until he was 22, but within four years he won the British featherweight title and then the WBO world crown. A dislocated shoulder later ruled him out of action for two years, but he returned to fight again. He is also heavily involved with the Professional Boxers Association.

BRITISH BOXING was at a low ebb when Colin McMillan prepared to challenge Italian Mauricio Stecca for the WBO world featherweight title. If ever the sport needed a crusader, a knight in shining armour to lift the sport from the gloom in which it was enveloped, it was now. The echoes of the tragic injuries to Michael Watson, in his ill-fated fight with Chris Eubank eight months before, still rumbled on. A series of mismatches, some grotesque, had done nothing to raise the morale or lift the image of the old game. Then just three days before McMillan's date with destiny, his great friend and sparring partner, Duke McKenzie, had lost his WBO bantamweight title, being knocked out inside a round by Rafael Del Valle of Puerto Rico. 'I watched that fight on television, in my hotel room. And I couldn't believe what I saw,' remembered McMillan. 'We had sparred dozens of rounds together, helping each other to prepare. And Duke had been in prime form. When I saw what happened to him, it made the omens look bleak for me. I could have wept for Duke. We had been close pals for years. I would have been at ringside to support him if I did not have such a big fight coming up myself. But it was not what I wanted to see, from my personal point of view either. You want to see and hear only good news, to put you in the right frame of mind. Nothing negative.'

So McMillan was uneasy as he endured the countdown to his match with Stecca, at London's Alexandra Palace on 16 May 1992. He had another cause for concern as well, notwithstanding the fact that he was due to face a man who had been an Olympic champion and whose strength and power had earned him victory in all bar one of his 46 professional fights. For McMillan was a perennial sufferer from hay fever – and the weather was unseasonably hot and humid in London for late spring. 'I just hoped and prayed that I wouldn't go down with it,' he said. 'But it was lurking in the back of my mind all the time.'

Fortunately, there was not a sneeze or a sniffle in sight as he stepped into the ring to face Stecca. Now the man dubbed the boxing boffin was ready to put his theories to the acid test. McMillan had left school with seven O-levels and three A-levels and he had initially let boxing take a back seat as he pursued his main career as a laboratory technician. Only when he passed all his qualification examinations did he turn to the sport in a full-time capacity. His views on boxing were somewhat studious, too. 'I always wanted to show that it's not all about beating people into submission, that boxing is a skill, that you can win by stealth as much as by just punching power,' he said. 'People said I didn't have sufficient power to become a world champion because a lot of my opponents went the distance. What they didn't realise is that I was fighting good, genuine opponents, many of them heavier than me. I've known of too many boxers who have been fed a diet of outclassed opposition, knocked them all over – but then been unprepared and unschooled when it came to the real challenge. I was always determined that wouldn't happen to me. And the men around me were of the same opinion. That's why I knew I had the ability to beat Stecca.

'I had worked hard, like I always have, on two key elements – speed and timing. They would provide me with the tools to defeat Stecca. And I was straight into action from the start, not giving him any time to settle into his own rhythm.' Indeed, McMillan was a dancing master, his sharpness and quicksilver movement making the champion look flatfooted by comparison. Stecca kept trudging his way forward, only to be met by the stinging counters from McMillan's left hand. When he did connect with one powerful uppercut in one of the early rounds, the challenger proved himself a crafty psychologist as well. 'I said to him, "Good shot!" And he looked a bit taken aback by what I said. He thought he had hurt me – he had, to be honest! – but by applauding him I was suggesting I wasn't really hurt too much. It made him realise I was ready to take his best shots and that didn't do much for his confidence. That gave me a vital edge. So much of this game is about the mental side. If you have two fighters, both superbly fit and evenly matched, it's generally the one who comes out on top mentally who wins.'

How true those words were to prove, as Stecca could ruefully testify. The tough, streetwise Italian had fought in seven previous world title fights, his relentless brand of pressure earning him victory in all bar one. But never before had an opponent had the cheek to compliment him on a punch. And this guy actually smiled as he said it! Stecca tried mightily to steal the initiative in the middle rounds, but McMillan would simply not be denied. By the final bell, the arms raised by the champion were surely no more than a gesture of defiance. Surely we had a new king to salute.

Then the MC announced the verdict . . . a split decision. 'That was the first time in the night when I felt a sense of panic. I knew I had won the fight – but was I about to be robbed of my triumph? I knew enough about dubious decisions over the years not to take anything for granted,' said McMillan. Thankfully, two of the judges had scored the fight to McMillan by margins of seven and eight rounds. The third judge had given the verdict to the Italian by a two-point margin, amid howls of outrage from the audience. It was discovered, an hour later, that the judge's card had been added up incorrectly and, in fact, he had McMillan two points ahead.

There was delirium in McMillan's dressing-room as the media and the fans saluted the new champion. It was a performance to uplift the battered spirit of boxing. We had a man who seemed destined to reign for years, a stylist who evoked cherished memories of that other great featherweight craftsman of an earlier era, Howard Winstone.

'Please don't start comparing me with legends like that. Wait till my career is over before you judge me,' McMillan pleaded with reporters. How sadly prophetic those words would prove. In his first defence, against Colombian Ruban Palacio just four months later, the champion dislocated his right shoulder and was forced to abdicate his crown. For two long years he endured a series of operations before returning to the ring again.

At the time of going to print, it remains doubtful if the gifted McMillan will ever be able to recapture that old magic. But he will always be remembered as the man who became a champion for the cause of British boxing . . . when we most needed one.

The Old Man Bounces Back

Archie Moore v Yvon Durelle

Archie Moore was born in Benoit, Mississippi, on 13 December 1916 – or was it 1913, as his mother always claimed? Moore himself insists she added three years to his age! Although he began boxing professionally in 1935, it was not until 1952 that he was finally granted a challenge at the world light heavyweight title, which he won by outpointing Joey Maxim. He held the title for eight years before it was stripped from him. He also fought twice for the world heavyweight title, but was knocked out first by Rocky Marciano and then by Floyd Patterson. He finally retired in 1962.

THEY CALLED him Ageless Archie Moore – and no wonder! Nobody ever quite knew just how old the man from Mississippi really was. Although he has long maintained that he was born in 1916, his mother swore, right till she went to her grave, that he came into this world three years sooner. Moore contents himself with a wide smile when the question is raised nowadays. It is more likely that his mother was telling the truth and that Archie Moore took three years off his age to make him appear a little more youthful.

If we take Momma's word, Moore was 39 years old and had been fighting professionally for 17 years before he finally managed to win a challenge at the world light heavyweight title he had coveted for so long. Politics had kept him out in the cold. His ferocious punching power had earned him a feared reputation as a knockout specialist – and that made the champions wary as he tried, without success, right through the 1940s to get his title chance. But Moore was a firebrand out of the ring as well and that hardly helped his cause.

Remember that Moore came from a time and from a part of America's deep south where slavery had been abolished barely half a century before. The mistrust between black and white still persisted. That had bitten even more deeply into relationships between black fighters and white managers. And Moore, always concerned that the men who guided his career might be helping themselves rather more than they were helping him, changed managers as regularly as Elizabeth Taylor swapped husbands. He had eight all told, some sacked with good reason, others treated with less than fairness. In the end it was one of the most famous managers in boxing's whole history, Jack 'Doc' Kearns, the man who helped ten world champions, including Jack Dempsey, to success, who gained him the title shot he wanted so badly – at a price. Kearns was manager of Joey Maxim, the champion of the time, and agreed to give Moore his chance – providing the challenger would hand Kearns a share of his contract. Moore reluctantly agreed – there was no other option open to him.

Moore outpointed Maxim to win the world crown on 17 December 1952 – four days past his 39th birthday if we take his mother's date. He had already had around 150 fights, winning all bar a handful, and he was destined never to lose another one in his rightful division for the next decade. The only contests he lost were to reigning world heavyweight champion Rocky Marciano; then, when Marciano retired, to Floyd Patterson for the vacant title; and finally, in 1962, against the blossoming talent of Cassius Clay. When Moore finally retired the following year he had lost his title outside the ring because of his inactivity.

It is true that in his quest for the heavyweight crown – boxing's Holy Grail – he had tended to brush aside his responsibilities to his own light heavyweight division In fact, he defended it a mere nine times in as many years. He was quite prepared to travel to wherever the big money was, coming to London to knock out Britain's top challenger, Yolande Pompey. But it was what originally seemed no more than a routine defence, against a tough but unheralded Canadian called Yvon Durelle, at the Montreal Forum on 10 December 1958, which he now regards as his finest hour – indeed, it has earned its place in boxing folklore as one of the most wildly fluctuating and spectacular world title fights of all.

'It was the kind of fight that every fighter would long to be in – as long as he emerged victorious,' says Moore. 'Every fighter dreams of being involved in a knockdown, drag-on kind of war – unless he's the eventual loser. I knew this was a fight that was always going to be remembered even as it was going on. I remember thinking to myself in the fifth round: "This must be fantastic for the fans out there watching."'

Moore, by that juncture, should really have been thanking his lucky stars, or his tremendous powers of recovery, for still being on his feet. He had been knocked off them three times in a sensational opening round when Durelle, the rank outsider, came steaming in to catch him totally unawares. 'I was surprised,' he admits. 'The first time I went down I said to myself: "Gee, this guy can really hit." When I went down the second time, I said to myself: "Gee, this guy can really, REALLY hit!"

'I was badly hurt in the first round. But I got myself together, then started dishing out some punishment of my own.' Moore was to crash to the floor for the fourth time in the fight in that fifth round, but he had also sent Durelle tumbling twice with mighty punches of his own as the fight moved its seesawing way into the 11th round. Moore's crouching, darting style had earned him the nickname The Mongoose. That style, allied to the growing authority of his punches against an opponent finally beginning to tire, had already begun to put the champion back in command. Now he was ready to launch his final strike.

'I was using my left hand a lot, picking him off. It was quite an educated punch and I knew it was working its cleverness on Yvon,' he said. 'He was such a game guy, but I figured he'd given it his best shot. Now I was ready to give mine.' Durelle, blood spurting from cuts on his nose and near his right eye, was hit with a mighty right hook which floored him. He had no right to beat the count, but he did, rising on legs that had already signalled surrender as the referee reached nine. But another piledriving right hand from the champion sent him crashing again. He rolled over on his back, seemingly unconscious, as the formality of the count began. Somehow the Canadian found a vestige of resistance somewhere in his subconscious to make a gallant attempt to rise again but he was still on his knees as he was counted out.

'I knew we'd both been in a special kind of fight,' said Moore. So did the audience, who had gone through every emotional gambit with the two fighters and were by this stage totally drained themselves. The contest also aroused so much excited interest on television in the USA that public demand for a rematch led to them meeting again eight months later, at the same venue. But the Durelle that turned up this time was a pale shadow of the challenger who had come so close to sensational triumph the first time. Moore took him apart before knocking him out in the third round. It was the kind of disappointing sequel which more often than not follows an epic encounter. But nobody can take away from either man the lasting and thrilling legacy of their first meeting.

Vengeance of a Tortured Man

Floyd Patterson v Ingemar Johansson

Floyd Patterson was born in Waco, North Carolina, on 4 January 1935. A brilliant amateur boxer, he won the gold medal at the age of 17 at the 1952 Olympic Games in Helsinki before turning professional. He became the youngest world heavyweight champion – a record later bettered by Mike Tyson – when, aged 21 years and ten months, he stopped veteran Archie Moore in five rounds to win the title vacated by Rocky Marciano's retirement in 1956. After losing the title to Sweden's Ingemar Johansson he defeated his conqueror in a rematch to create another record as the first former heavyweight champion to regain his title.

FOR A WHOLE YEAR, minus six days, Floyd Patterson was a man gripped by personal torment. It would be foolish to expect any fighter to accept defeat with a smile, especially when the loss of a world title is involved. But few losers have ever sunk to the extraordinary depths of despair to which Patterson succumbed after losing his world heavyweight crown to Ingemar Johansson in New York on 26 June 1959. The European challenger might have been champion of his own continent but he was written off by the Americans. After all, apart from a couple of brief interludes back in the '30s, when Italian Primo Carnera and German Max Schmeling had 'borrowed' the title, it had remained in North American hands right the way through the century. Johansson was a Swede – whoever heard of a Swedish heavyweight? Ingo was also written off as a playboy, who was only in New York to take away a few dollars.

After all, while all real fighters lock themselves away in solitude as they prepare for the big day, this guy had booked a suite in one of the city's swankiest hotels. He had even brought over a gorgeous Swedish dame to share his quarters! The guy was only here for the ride.

It was an image Johansson had carefully cultivated, to lure Patterson into a similar sense of complacency. Sure, he was a devotee of the bright lights and the clubs – when he wasn't in training. But he had prepared for this opportunity as arduously as any challenger ever did back in his native Sweden. He had stopped Britain's two top heavyweights, Joe Erskine and Henry Cooper, to retain his European title, and he had knocked out American Eddie Machen, a long-time challenger for Patterson's crown, inside a round to become the top-ranked challenger in the influential *Ring* magazine. He certainly boasted stronger credentials than the disappointingly small 18,000 crowd at the Yankee Stadium gave him.

He also possessed a right hand known throughout Europe as Ingo's Bingo or The Hammer of Thor . . . a mighty punch that had stopped 13 of his 20 opponents in his unbeaten career. For two rounds that right hand could have been tied behind his back as he poked and prodded out his left jab against a champion whose all-round purpose and work-rate won him both rounds with ease. Then suddenly, in the opening minute of the third round, Johansson flicked out another left – and followed up with a crunching right, straight into the champion's face. It caught Patterson on the mouth, but the force was enough to stun him as he tumbled to the floor. He was still in obvious distress as he hauled himself up at the count of nine – and went to walk to a neutral corner. 'I got hit so hard that when I heard the referee counting I assumed I had knocked him down,' he said. Another punishing right hand sent him crashing again. 'Again I didn't know I was on the floor. I remember looking out of the ring at the timekeeper and there, sat right next to him was John Wayne. I thought, "Oh, my goodness, that's John Wayne!" Then I realised I was looking at him from a funny angle – that I was on the floor.'

Again he climbed up, only to be smashed down and down again – a total of seven times in all before referee Ruby Goldstein finally halted the carnage. As Johansson and his camp celebrated, Patterson could feel only self-disgust. 'I felt I had let my country down, letting someone come from another country and take the title,' he said. 'I had just come off another fight the previous month and I never gave myself the chance to rest. I'm making no excuses, but I was way over-trained.'

Thus started Patterson's year in his self-made hell. 'I went into hiding, I just felt ashamed. I didn't go out much, but when I did I wore a false moustache and beard so the people couldn't recognise me. I guess I became a kind of hermit.' His hideaway was in the sanctuary of the Catskill Mountains in upstate New York. His mentor was Cus D'Amato, who had moved to the sleepy little backwater as his own refuge from the hoodlums and gangsters who had controlled boxing in New York in the early 1950s. Just as Mike Tyson was to follow the same trail a generation later, Patterson had gone to join D'Amato's commune as a way of salvaging his life after becoming a problem child in his early teens. D'Amato had coaxed, cajoled and guided him all the way to that world title. Now he used those same powers to pick up the pieces of the fallen champion – and rebuild him into an even more formidable fighting force.

D'Amato's major task was to transform the self-loathing inside his charge into a supercharged desire to regain his title. 'Freudian Floyd', one wag had christened Patterson, so intense and so complex was his mind. But D'Amato worked his magic again and by the time he had completed an intensive two months at his training camp, Patterson's condition was perfect – physically and, more to the point, mentally. 'I had desire – and I had fear,' he said. 'I knew Johansson could hurt me bad – he had done so in that first fight. Maybe before then I had not felt fear. Now I did – and fear is absolutely essential in boxing because when you have that inside you it does something to you. It makes you faster, stronger. Because I had that fear it made me feel good – I knew I was going to fight my kind of fight. I never said I was going to win the title back. But I did know that I was going to give him a tough fight. And if they raised his hand in victory at the end, he was going to have difficulty getting it up.'

The return was in New York again, this time at the Polo Grounds on 20 June 1960. Seven former champions had attempted a similar mission but, to this point in history, nobody had ever regained sport's supreme prize before. So this time Johansson was the overwhelming favourite. How could Patterson defy history when the likes of Joe Louis and Jack Dempsey had failed? But right from the opening bell, Patterson was a man transformed. There was a bristling, almost brutal aggression about him which had never been seen before.

Johansson was forced constantly back, never able to cope with the speed, the mobility and the hurtful punches from the challenger, never able to set himself up for his own big right hand. Patterson was blessed with phenomenal hand speed – at his peak those hands were like pistons, even faster than Muhammad Ali's. The punches raining in on him must have seemed like a blurred nightmare to the outclassed Swede. For four rounds the remorseless punishment continued. Then, in round five, with the fickle audience now firmly on Patterson's side, now roaring for the former champion, a sweeping left hook – Floyd's favourite and most damaging punch – landed flush on Johansson's jaw. He toppled over, rising unsteadily as the count reached nine. But Sweden's all-time sporting hero was fast losing his hold on the title the Americans always considered as their own property.

This may have been Patterson's day of atonement, but it was America's party. The crowd were screaming now as Patterson came calmly out of a neutral corner and sent Johansson crashing again with another perfectly executed left hook. This time there was never the remotest possibility of the champion beating the count. Indeed, he had not moved, he was totally unconscious. Suddenly, Patterson's celebrations were cut short. He had thrown his arms joyously in the air at the moment of triumph. Now, seeing Johansson prostrate, he feared that punch might have inflicted serious damage. He ran to the stricken Swede and, kneeling beside him, saw blood trickling from the corner of his mouth. For a few seconds he feared Johansson was seriously hurt. But then, thankfully, his body began to move as his brain started to focus again.

The pair were to fight for a third time nine months later in Miami Beach, when Patterson, twice on the floor in the opening round, came back to knock down Johansson before that round was over and eventually knocked him out in the sixth. So Patterson won the rubber 2–1 – the high point in the career of a man who was simply too small to be considered one of the great heavyweight champions. Patterson weighed barely 13 stone and that was tiny, even in an era far removed from the giant heavyweights of today. That sheer lack of bulk was eventually exposed when he was twice knocked out inside a round by the awesome Sonny Liston, who was just too big, too strong and too damned mean for one of the genuinely nicest men ever to grace the sport. 'But I wouldn't change a thing in my whole life,' says Patterson. 'I've been through it all. And when I look back, I'm happy with myself now. That's what's most important.'

Tears of a Crown

Robbie Regan v Daniel Jiminez

Robbie Regan was born in Caerphilly, just north of Cardiff, on 30 August 1968. He turned professional just before his 21st birthday and won the British flyweight title in only his eighth contest. He went on to win the European title, relinquishing and then regaining the belt, before being beaten by Mexican Alberto Jiminez in his challenge for the WBO world flyweight title. He moved up to bantamweight to finally achieve his world title ambition by outpointing WBO champion Daniel Jiminez of Puerto Rico.

NO TRIUMPH in the whole history of boxing in Wales carried the emotional overtones of Robbie Regan's pulsating victory over Puerto Rico's Daniel Jiminez at Cardiff's Sophia Gardens on the night of 26 April 1996. The tears of jubilation flowed from the dynamic little Welshman as the WBO world bantamweight belt he had so courageously plundered from a fine champion was strapped around his waist. The eyes of his manager, Dai Gardiner, were also moist as he sat in the new champion's dressing-room an hour later, the haunting memories of 16 years before flooding back. It was a poignant moment as the ecstasy of victory had slowly began to subside, the crowded, noisy celebrations replaced by an almost sombre mood of reflection.

'I feel like an old man,' said Regan as he eventually rose stiffly and painfully from his chair. 'My face is sore, I can hardly lift my arms and my feet are killing me. And I feel so dehydrated it's going to take me another hour or more before I can manage a sample for my urine test. That's what I call winning a world title the hard way. But no pain in the world can hide the pride I feel inside me. I'm the champion of the world. They can never take it away from me now, can they?' The final question was almost a plea for reassurance from the newly crowned champion, as if some fear still lurked in his mind that someone would snatch his glory from him.

It was easy to understand that niggling worry. Twice in the previous ten months Regan had been struck by numbing despair in his almost lifelong quest to win the world title on which he had set his heart since he first walked into a gym, a tiny 11-year-old waif. That was back in 1980, a year that will forever be a harrowing memory to the manager sat silently beside him. Dai Gardiner had another brilliant Welsh bantamweight prospect at that time. His name was Johnny Owen, who went all the way to Los Angeles to challenge the powerful Mexican Lupe Pintor for the WBC world title. Owen boxed brilliantly for half the fight, before finally being caught by the champion's merciless onslaught in the later rounds. The challenger was eventually knocked out in the 12th round – and never regained consciousness, dying in hospital some days later.

Gardiner had sat distraught at poor Owen's bedside, watching the life trickling slowly away from the young man he had brought to America with so much hope. In his remorse, he had decided to walk away from the sport which had been his life since his own fighting days. Then friends, urging him to return, cajoled him into watching this young boy Regan who was already bringing fresh excitement to the valleys. 'I went to watch him train – and I was hooked again,' says Gardiner. 'Nothing could ever take away the memory of Johnny Owen, but I felt I owed it to Johnny – and to myself – to take another boy from the area and try to carry him that one stage further.'

So began the hazardous journey that seemed to reach a shuddering end in Cardiff in June 1995, when Regan was retired by his own corner after a bruising nine rounds challenge to Mexican Alberto Jiminez for the WBO world flyweight title. There were tears from Robbie that night as well – tears of bitter frustration. 'I'm not one for making excuses, but I should never have fought that night,' he said. The contest had already been postponed twice when first Regan and then Jiminez went down with illness. Then, a few weeks before the twice rescheduled date, Regan had to undergo surgery for damage to knuckles on his left hand.

'They warned me I should rest the hand for weeks and not think about fighting for a few months. But I was desperate. If I pulled out again, the fight might never have taken place – and I might have never got another chance,' he said. So Regan battled on, his left hand becoming more painful with every round. 'When I finally took the bandages off in my dressing-room, the skin had been ripped off the knuckles, the cut was so deep that you could see the knuckle-bone,' he said. He feared the hand had been so badly damaged that he might never be able to punch with it again. But luckily, after another operation, the surgeon told me the hand would heal – as long as I rested it for three months. This time I did exactly what he told me,' said Regan.

It was just before Christmas that year when he fought again. He was given another chance at a cherished world title, this time facing unbeaten Tunisian Ferid Ben Jeddou for the IBF interim flyweight crown. The opportunity came because American champion Danny Romero had been forced to temporarily vacate the title after suffering a serious injury in training. Regan was at his blistering best, blasting his opponent to defeat inside two rounds. It seemed that his ambition had finally been realised. But the IBF, who had already been paid their sanctioning fee, then reneged on their decision and declared the title vacant.

'I was devastated, I just couldn't believe what was happening,' said Regan. 'Dai and promoter Frank Warren were ready to make an appeal, but I had started to wonder whether I was fated never to be a world champion. Then, out of the blue, the chance came to fight Daniel Jiminez for the WBO world bantamweight title. It meant I would have to go up six pounds from flyweight, but that didn't bother me at all. I was grateful for it in some ways. Getting those last few ounces off to get down to eight stone is sheer hell. I always have to dehydrate myself for 24 hours before a weigh-in, to get the fluid out of my body. This time I knew I would be nice and strong.'

Regan's plan was to use that extra strength against a champion who was an artful dodger in the ring but lacked real firepower. Jiminez had already fought three times in Britain, outsmarting Duke McKenzie to win the WBO world super bantamweight title, then, after he lost that crown, returning to capture the bantamweight belt from African Alfred Kotey and proving too sharp for Scot Drew Docherty. 'I knew I had to change my usual tactics, to hustle and bustle him, get in close to him.'

For the first two rounds Jiminez's sharp left jab and his nimble footwork kept the challenger at bay. But this was a night when

Regan would not be denied. He forced his way back into contention by sheer willpower. As he anticipated, his heavier punching nullified much of the champion's elegant but often ineffective counters. 'He was a clever so and so, but he never really put me under pressure,' said Robbie. By the sixth round, the halfway stage, Regan had battled back to such a degree that the fight was even. Then, after Jiminez had danced his way to winning the seventh, the real turning point came in the following round.

Regan had stalked his quarry for the whole round, finally trapping him on the ropes with the seconds running out. He unleashed a thunderous left hand which caught the champion perfectly on the jaw, sending him toppling over to the canvas, his eyes betraying the dazed state of his mind. The count seemed an interminably long one before Jiminez finally clambered to his feet as American referee Veno Rodrigues reached nine. Precious seconds more were lost as the referee slowly wiped his gloves and asked him if he was ready to continue. By the time Jiminez could nod his head, the bell had rung to end the round. 'Another half a minute or so and I would have stopped him there and then. He was really hurt,' said Regan.

But the knockdown had sent Regan soaring ahead for the first time. Now he had four more rounds to grit his teeth, ignore the tiredness that was beginning to seep through his body, and keep his attacking momentum. Jiminez battled from equal desperation. He knew his title was on the line. It made for an absorbing finale, with champion and challenger giving everything to their respective causes. But if Jiminez landed more punches, it was Regan who continued to carry the heavier artillery. He had also the support of a crowd who were on their feet in the excitement, screaming him on. 'It gives you that vital little extra lift to hear them,' he said.

At the end all three judges had Regan ahead – two by margins of three rounds and one by an astonishing five. It was far, far closer than that. But even Jiminez, as graceful in defeat as he had been in defence, acknowledged the fairness of the decision. 'You are a true champion,' he told Regan. 'Maybe we have another fight . . .'

'Maybe we will, one day,' said Regan later. 'But right now I just want to savour the moment, enjoy it, perhaps take a little holiday before I think about fighting again. This fight has changed my life. If I had lost this time, I don't think I would have been able to carry on in boxing. You can only take so many setbacks in one life. I honestly don't think I could have coped with losing again.'

As for Dai Gardiner, having finally guided a Welshman to a world bantamweight title, his mind was a whirl of emotions. 'It's a long, long road we've finally ended,' he said. 'I feel so happy for Robbie because if any man has earned a world title he has. And I guess that somewhere up there [raising his eyes to heaven] dear Johnny Owen will be applauding, too.'

Once in a Lifetime

Ed Robinson v Lee Simpkin

Edwin Robinson was born in Taplow, Berkshire, on 21 October 1971. He learned to box while at boarding school and had 25 amateur contests, winning 'about half'. He had his one and – he pledges – only professional contest in 1996.

IT WAS WELL AFTER 11 o'clock at night. Only one contest was left on a long evening's boxing at London's Elephant and Castle Leisure Centre. It would normally present a scene of desolation. Apart from a few family members and friends, only a handful of hardened fans remain to the bitter end of small-hall shows. But this night, 2 April 1996, was astoundingly different. The majority of a packed house remained in their seats for the finale. And as Ed Robinson made his way from the squash court that had been commandeered as a temporary dressing-room to the ringside, he was given the kind of hysterical reception normally reserved for world champions.

Looking pale, tense and totally concentrated, he stood briefly a few feet away from the ring as at least 150 of his supporters broke from their seats and laid siege to the ringside, screaming their loyalty. Most had never been to a boxing match in their lives before this night. But many of them proudly wore their 'Ed Case' badges. Girls and boys together, all twentysomethings, yuppies, young City types, college kids, ex-boarding school pals, a smattering of amateur fighters – this was Ed's Army, a noisy, happy, barmy army, the like of which has surely never been encountered at a British ringside before. 'Just about every friend I ever had was there. To see them, to hear them making all that noise . . . it was overwhelming. I'll never have another night in my whole life quite like that one,' says Robinson.

It was a night that also marked the culmination of a dream for the 24-year-old Robinson who, a couple of years previously, had proudly left University College, London, bearing a Bachelor of Science (Honours) degree in Progressive Management for Consumers. 'Some students take a year out after college to back-pack around the world. I decided to take a break by doing something in the boxing world, just as a bit of an adventure,' he said. 'I'd always been fascinated by the sport. Until I was 15, I wasn't able to play any sport because I suffered from asthma and hay fever. But when I went to Bradfield College Sixth Form Boarding School the illnesses cleared up. I was able to play a bit of rugby. And I decided to learn to box – I was pretty small for my age and I wanted to make sure I wouldn't be bullied.'

Robinson went to nearby Reading Amateur Boxing Club, where he was coached by former pro Austen Owens, 'a great bloke for whom nothing was too much trouble. He's the man who really won me over to the sport.' Ed ended up boxing 25 amateur contests, 'never setting the world alight. I lost as many as I won. But it was a marvellous way of getting fit. And there was a great camaraderie about it all. A true amateur spirit.' On leaving university, he applied for a post as press officer with Panix Promotions, a London-based boxing organisation funded by Panos Eliades, a wealthy businessman, and spearheaded by Frank Maloney, manager of the reigning WBC world heavyweight champion Lennox Lewis and also one of the sport's busiest promoters. Maloney gave him the job. 'I like to employ university graduates. They're intelligent. And I reckon a few years in this game finishes off their education!' he says.

Robinson was captivated by the strange new world of the pro game. 'Being on the inside in all the political side of things, mixing with the fighters, organising press conferences, meeting the press, travelling . . . I just loved the whole scene,' he said. 'But it was the fighters I looked up to most of all. Going into that ring, with all the risks and dangers involved – they're all brave men. Gradually, the urge began to grow inside me to have a go at it myself, just to sample what it was like. Then I would be able to talk to the boxers, if not on the same level then at least as someone who had experienced it for myself.'

The knockout that stunned the world – Buster Douglas destroys Mike Tyson

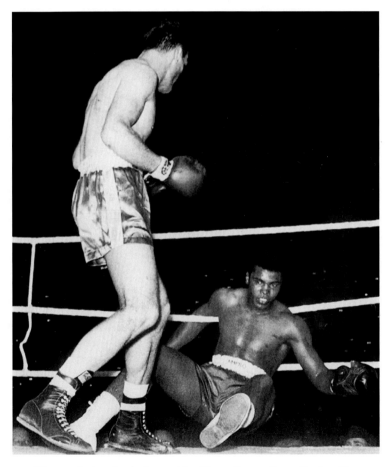

The punch that shook the world – Henry Cooper floors Cassius Clay

But that famous mouth did not stay shut for long

It wasn't long before Tyson was working up a lather again

Lift off . . . for Herbie Hide

Gerald McClellan has Nigel Benn on the ropes

But now it is the American who is in distress

. . . and Benn celebrates

A gathering of great champions, from left Colin McMillan, Charlie Magri, Ken Buchanan, Howard Winstone and John H. Stracey

John Conteh aims a playful punch at singer Grace Jones, while George Melly referees

Pensive moments from Marvin Hagler (left) and Sugar Ray Leonard

If the crown fits . . . Naseem Hamed tries it for size

Robinson put the idea to Maloney, who reluctantly agreed. 'It's a tough game and I didn't want to see him get hurt,' he said. For six weeks Robinson cut himself off from all the social pleasures a high-spirited 24-year-old living with a group of pals in London would enjoy. 'I ran every morning, did my job in the day, then trained in the evenings,' he said. 'I trained at the Thomas A'Beckett gym under Colin Wilson, who was brilliant. And the pros I sparred with were very helpful as well. I got my licence to box from the British Boxing Board, then had to have a thorough medical check with Dr Walsh. I'd met him before through taking boxers to be checked over. Now it was my turn. I said to him, "You think I'm mad, don' t you?" He looked back at me and said: "Son, you only live this life once and then you die . . ." I knew exactly what he meant. We take risks in life every day – even driving a car to work. People are naturally self-destructive. A lot of people I know take drugs. Others I remember from college days used to get drunk out of their minds every night. The average life expectancy of a Sumo wrestler is 45. When you look at all that, is boxing any more dangerous?'

The great day finally dawned for Robinson with two worries clouding his mind. His original opponent, former Welsh amateur international Wesley Jones, had been forced to withdraw through illness. Such problems are part and parcel of down-the-bill fights on small-hall shows, and matchmaker Dean Powell managed to find a substitute, Lee Simpkin from Swadlincote in Derbyshire, who was prepared to box at 24 hours' notice. The most vexing concern for Ed, though, concerned his mother, Margaret. 'I had not dared to tell her I was having a professional fight,' he confessed. 'She didn't like me fighting as an amateur. She hates the sport. I don't know how she would have reacted if she had known what I was doing. So I decided that the safest thing was not to tell her.'

Simpkin, though little more than a novice himself, weighed in at 11 stone 8½lbs when he arrived – far heavier than Robinson who was exactly on the light-middleweight limit of 11 stone. 'I was just pleased, however, that Dean had managed to find an opponent. The worst thing was having to wait around until the very last fight,' he said. Robinson had spent £20 on a pair of eye-popping pink shorts: 'I chose that colour as a bit of a laugh, to help persuade people not to take it all too seriously,' he said. That was one of the smaller bills he had to pay. 'I was paid £600 for the fight, but I paid out £250 in medical fees, £100 to my trainer, £10 to my cuts man, £30 for the licence, £60 for a pair of boots, £20 for the shorts and around £50 to use the gym. Add the cost of health foods and vitamins I took and I barely broke even. But that wasn't the important thing. No money could buy the excitement of that night,' he said.

Against a bigger and more rugged opponent, Robinson's tactic was to keep the fight at long range, to use his jab to frustrate the onrushing Simpkin and pile up the points for himself. Urged on by his increasingly frenzied supporters, he played out his plan to perfection in the first three rounds. With one more round to go, he had already built up a massive lead. But blood had begun to trickle from a cut on his nose at the end of the third. And there was an increasingly – and natural – tiredness about his work in the fourth. He had never been this far before. Simpkin, sensing a victory that had seemed highly unlikely, tried to pile on the pressure in the final three minutes. But that baying crowd almost willed their man through the ordeal of the closing seconds. There was no question of the winner at the end, and as Ed's right hand was raised in triumph, the ringside screams became pure ecstasy.

The victorious army celebrated long into the night at the Hanover Grand nightclub in the West End. It was a hungover hero who arrived an hour late for work the following morning, faintly embarrassed by the congratulatory telephone calls that kept interrupting his work-flow. 'That's it for me, I've had my moment and now I'm retiring. I'll never fight again,' he said. 'But it was an experience I will never forget. I told you that I've become hooked on boxing. I think I want to stay in it now as a career. Perhaps on the production side on television – that would be fascinating.'

Robinson's story, his Greatest Fight, is far removed from the glitz and the glamour of most of the treasured memories in this book. The high altars of boxing at Las Vegas and at Wembley, the rapturous glory of world title belts . . . like the majority of us, he will be merely an onlooker at such celebrated occasions. But his story is here to represent the thousands of boxers around this earth who are the real backbone of the sport. Their purses will never sound like telephone numbers. Most never make it beyond the six- or eight-round status. Yet by the simple act of stepping into a ring, each and every one of them is a hero, a brave man. Ed Robinson will vouch for that. But please don't let his mother know.

The Pie and Chips Champion

Steve Robinson v John Davison

Steve Robinson was born in Cardiff on 17 December 1968. He was more interested in football as a schoolboy and did not take up boxing until his late teens. He had no amateur experience before he launched his professional career on 1 March – St David's Day! – 1989. He won the Welsh featherweight title and then the Penta-Continental title before winning the WBO world title on 17 April 1993. He successfully defended the crown for a record seven times, before losing to Naseem Hamed two and a half years later.

STEVE ROBINSON had just finished his lunch of pie and chips when the telephone rang. His trainer, Ronnie Rush, was breathlessly excited on the other end of the line. And it was no small wonder. For it was a call that was to dramatically change both their lives. 'It's your big chance, Steve. You've got a shot at the world title,' he told him. 'That's brilliant, Ronnie. When?' he asked him. 'The day after tomorrow!' It was an answer that left Robinson stunned. 'No punch I ever took hit me like that. I could have fainted in disbelief. I just stammered a few words back at Ronnie and put the phone down. My hands were trembling. I was in a state of shock,' recalls Robinson.

An astonishing and tragic series of circumstances had combined to give Robinson the kind of break all fighters dream of. He was a 24-year-old from Cardiff's tough Ely council estate who had not turned to boxing until long after he left school. 'I saw it as a way of keeping fit, being able to look after myself – and making a few quid,' he said. 'Because I was a late developer I didn't bother with an amateur career at all. I just went straight in as a pro when I was 20.'

A tough learning experience it had been for the modest and mild-mannered Robinson. He lost no fewer than nine of his first 23 fights, establishing a reputation as a fighter who was strong and fit but really no more than a journeyman. 'Despite the record, I knew I was better than that. People forgot that I was starting from absolute scratch. But I was learning all the time, getting better with every fight,' he said. 'I was also having most of my fights in the other guy's backyard, often at short notice. I reckon I won at least half those fights where I didn't get the decision, but you learn to accept that. In a close fight it's the home-town boy who normally wins. So I was not too despondent about the way things were going.'

But financially life was tough for Steve and his long-time girlfriend (now his wife) Angela. The couple had only recently moved out of her parents' house to set up home with their baby son in a rented flat. Steve had taken a big gamble just two weeks earlier by giving up his job as a £58-a-week warehouseman to concentrate full time on boxing. 'I knew that if I was to get to the top I had to give everything to the sport,' he says. Now, with dramatic suddenness, that gamble was about to pay off. Two days to prepare for the biggest fight of your life, however, was mind-blowing. 'When I told Angie, she thought I was crazy to even think of taking the fight. And when I stopped to think seriously about it, she was probably right,' recalls Robinson. 'But if I didn't take the chance, who knows if another one would ever come along? That's what Ronnie Rush and my manager Dai Gardiner told me. And between them they convinced me that I could do it.

'Luckily I'm the kind of guy who always keeps himself pretty fit, so I reckoned I was about 80 per cent fit for it. I decided to give it a go. After all, nothing ventured means nothing gained. I trained in the gym that night and felt that I was at least ready to give it my best shot. In some ways it was an advantage having so little time. At least it meant I didn't have any time on my hands to worry about it all.'

Robinson had to travel 340 miles to the North-east of England to face Geordie John Davison for the vacant WBO world featherweight title in Washington on 17 April 1993. Davison, a rough and rugged campaigner, had been due to challenge the champion, Colombian Ruben Palacio. The veteran South American had caused a major upset for British boxing the previous year by plundering the crown from Colin McMillan, the skilled craftsman we had all expected to rule the world for many years. McMillan had dislocated his shoulder midway through the fight, leaving himself only one arm to fight with – an impossible task which forced his corner to retire him. If that defeat was a numbing blow for the sport, it paled compared to the shattering news three days before Palacio was due to face Davison. Like all overseas boxers who come to this country to fight, Palacio had to undertake a mandatory AIDS test. Tragically, he was discovered to have contracted the HIV virus. Promoters Barry Hearn and Tommy Gilmour had the onerous task of revealing the news to him and arranging for him to return to his own country with all possible haste. They were then left with a major television date to fill, but only one fighter – and just 72 hours to find an opponent. In desperation, they contacted several managers throughout the country, trying to find a substitute who was both fit and plausible. Robinson fitted that bill. He was always in good condition, they knew that, and he did hold the Welsh and Penta-Continental titles, which gave his name at least some credibility when they put it to the WBO representatives. In such dire circumstances, the WBO agreed, though it did seem to most observers that they were handing the crown to Davison on a proverbial plate. Robinson would be strong enough to give him a decent challenge, and it would at least keep the television moguls happy. Meanwhile, Geordieland could celebrate only their second world champion. That, at least, was the scenario.

But the quiet man from Cardiff had dreams of his own as he hurried to the local airport on the Friday morning, en route to the North-east. 'I didn't sleep very much on the Thursday night because I was so excited,' he said. 'Once the initial shock began to wear off, I started to realise that this was a chance from heaven for me. I felt very sad for Palacio – you don't wish that kind of thing on your worst enemy. But you have to take every advantage when something like this comes up.

'I knew plenty about Davison. He was a pretty tough, competitive fighter, with bags of heart and energy. But I reckoned I had more skill than him. I was the better boxer. Dai Gardiner and Ronnie Rush kept drumming that fact into me. I came face to face with Davison for the first time at the weigh-in and he seemed very tense and uptight. That was a good sign. I was feeling surprisingly loose and confident.

'I knew the crowd would be pretty hostile, but that didn't worry me when I got into the ring. By now I knew I had nothing to lose, everything to gain. I was ready for war.'

Robinson began like a man on fire, knocking Davison right out of his stride with his brand of bustle and guile. Roared on by his home-town fans, Davison tried in vain to land his big punches on an opponent who was repeatedly beating him to the jab, then moving out of range or covering up and taking his punches on his shoulders and arms.

'I knew I'd done well in the first four rounds or so. But then I began to feel a bit tired. I think it all caught up with me for a few rounds after that – and he came right back into the fight,' recalled Robinson. 'But then I got my second wind. I got over my rough patch; I started feeling good again. By the last three or four rounds I felt like I was walking on air. I felt so good, so strong, as if I was just being swept along to the title. I could hear the crowd screaming for Davison, but I knew I was ahead. He was game right up to the final bell. He kept coming forward, still trying to land the punch that could change the whole fight. But I could sense he was getting more and more desperate, as if he knew he was too far behind to catch me.

'I just kept pushing out my jab, then keeping away from him. When that final round ended, I was so excited I couldn't keep still. I knew I'd won. My only fear was that the judges, perhaps influenced by the crowd, would give it to him. But they didn't – and then there was pandemonium in my corner as Ronnie, Dai and a few others started lifting me on their shoulders to celebrate. It was an unbelievable feeling, an emotion I will never forget.'

But what Steve did forget was to ring Angela back in Cardiff to tell her of his triumph. 'The fight was not on television until a couple of hours later, so Angie had no idea that I had won until then. I did promise I would ring her if I had the championship belt, but there was so much excitement, so many people crowding around, that I didn't have the chance.'

By the time the fight was being shown to the nation, Robinson was on his way back home – stretched out on the back seat of a minibus. 'There were no planes back that late at night and I wanted to get back to friends and family as soon as I could. Robbie Giles, who owned the minibus, had brought up a few fans, so the rest of us travelled back with them. It was a strange journey. Somebody had brought some beers to celebrate, so they were all having a drink. But I don't touch the stuff – never have. I didn't need it, mind. Just being champion of the world was intoxicating enough.'

Robinson was to hold on to that title for two and a half years, defending it seven times before finally losing it to Naseem Hamed. It earned him the kind of financial rewards he could never have dreamed of when he was fighting for £300 a time. A brand new detached house in one of Cardiff's most affluent suburbs is testimony to his success. 'I guess you really could call me boxing's Cinderella Man,' he smiles.

Bulldog in a Bullring

John H. Stracey v Jose Napoles

John H. Stracey was born in Bethnal Green, London, on 22 September 1950. A fine amateur, he boxed for Britain in the 1968 Olympic Games in Mexico City and turned professional the following year, after he had won the ABA lightweight title. Moving up to welterweight, he became British, European and then world champion.

THE FANATICAL FATHERS of fighting sons have been a somewhat mixed blessing for their offspring. Managers and trainers treat them, in the main, with a mixture of loathing and fear because they have discovered, all too often, how a father who naïvely believes he understands the sport can turn the head of a son brought up to believe that dad always knows best. But John H. Stracey's father, Dave, was a glowing exception. His very presence in Mexico City provided the inspiration for the chirpy Cockney from Bethnal Green to achieve one of the most remarkable upsets in world title fights in British boxing's long history.

'Dad, God bless him, turned up a few days before the fight. When I saw him I just knew the title was mine. I didn't give a damn what the rest of the world might think. He had so much faith in me that it just rubbed off on me,' says Stracey, who surely needed such a powerful motivation to guide him through what even his own people back in London had decided was Mission Impossible. Stracey's powerful punching had carried him to stunning stoppage success in his quest for the British and then the European welterweight crowns. But this date, 6 December 1975, was to bring a challenge altogether more awesome than anything he had ever undertaken before. Jose Napoles, with the exception of one little eight-month hiccough, had ruled the world welterweight picture with devastating power for nearly seven years. A native of Cuba, he had escaped Castro's regime to set up home in Mexico. The Mexicans had taken him to their hearts as he smashed his way through all who dared to seek his crown. His defences were staged in a bullring in Mexico City which he had turned into his own forbidding fortress, with 20,000 screaming supporters always in attendance, their frenzy adding to the challenger's ordeal. 'That's how it was the night I fought Napoles – 19,984 shouting and yelling for him and 16 people rooting for me!' recalls Stracey. 'But it didn't frighten me. I was a pretty confident guy to begin with. I knew that once the bell went it was only him and me. And besides, my dad was there. I wouldn't have swapped his support for all 19,984 who were against me.'

Because of his own aggressive style and the location of the fight, Stracey was christened the British Bulldog by the press. He gladly acceded to their request to be photographed draped in a Union Jack. 'It might sound corny, but I'm actually proud of being British. I always had a special buzz fighting for my country,' he said. He didn't have much of a buzz when he first arrived in Mexico City two weeks before the fight, however. 'It was the early hours of the morning when the plane touched down. We were all shattered after a long trip – and then the Mexicans who met us took us to our "hotel", which turned out to be nothing more than a shack,' he said. 'My manager Terry Lawless went spare and threatened to pull out of the fight there and then unless the accommodation was changed. He must have scared them. They took us straight off to the best hotel in the town. I can remember waking up after a few hours sleep and having breakfast out on the poolside, with all these gorgeous girls around the place. I don't know how much confidence Terry had in me, but I vividly remember him saying as he came and sat next to me: "If we're gonna be screwed, we're gonna be screwed in style!"'

While acclimatisation in the rarified atmosphere of Mexico's capital city is never easy, Stracey was fortunate in that he had trained and fought there seven years before, as the precocious 18-year-old baby of Britain's Olympic boxing team. 'I knew all about the problems with altitude, the lack of oxygen,' he said. 'I had to train even harder to be able to go 15 rounds at full pelt.'

After less than two minutes of the opening round, however, it seemed that all his exhausting preparation was only a sadly wasted effort. He was down on his knees, dumped there by a vicious left hook from a champion grimly determined to end his night's work early. 'There had been rumours that he was finding it harder and harder to make the weight – after all, he was 35, ten years older than me, and the older you get the harder it is to shed those last couple of pounds,' said Stracey. 'So we had prepared for him to come out throwing bombs, trying to catch me cold. But I hadn't planned for a start like this!' Stracey, in fact, did not even know he had been put down until he tottered back to his corner at the end of the opening round. 'To this day I don't remember a thing about it,' he said. 'I know I'm in the ring in there with him, then my mind goes blank. And when I come to, I'm in close with him again. It's only because I've seen it on television that I know the knockdown happened.'

Stracey had, in fact, survived a merciless beating from Napoles. He was to suffer another bruising three minutes in round two, as the champion continued his bombardment. 'He really was a class act, this guy. I can remember thinking that,' said Stracey. 'Then I remember going back to my corner at the end of the round, slumping in the stool and asking Terry Lawless how I was doing. "You're doing fine," he told me. "You must be joking – the guy ain't stopped hitting me," I said back to him. But then Terry almost made me grin. "Yeah, he's still hitting you but not so hard or with so many punches as in the first round!" he said.

'I don't know if Lawless was a master of psychology, but I went out there the very next round and started to take over the fight. I put him on the floor with a sharp left hook in that round – and, would you believe it, I froze. I didn't know quite what to do. I think that when he went down – this man was a legend remember, one of the greatest welterweight champions of all time – it shocked me. Here was I, 8,000 miles away from home, within a punch of destroying this legend. By the time it had all sunk in, he was back on his feet and clutching me, giving himself precious extra seconds to recover.'

But while the fading Napoles bought himself some temporary relief, his time was running out. Stracey was at his bulldog best in rounds four and five, smashing punches into the champion's face, opening cuts around both eyes. The Mexicans were stunned into near silence by now. Even with a Mexican referee and three Mexican judges, there was nothing to stop Stracey's relentless march. The end came in round six, when Napoles had been reduced to a shambling, beaten-up shadow of a once-great champion. He looked every one of his years as the slaughter was eventually stopped.

As the few Britons around the ring celebrated joyously, the Mexicans were generous in their applause for a new champion. 'They gave me a real salute,' said Stracey. 'Mind, there must have been about 25 people who invaded the ring at the end, all shaking my hand. But with their other hand they nicked my dressing-gown, my towelling, even my gumshield.

'I guess it was a small price to pay for the unbelievable feeling of knowing that you're world champion – and you've beaten a great fighter to win it. The man I most wanted to see was my dad – we both had tears in our eyes as we celebrated, I can tell you that. He'd been there at the back of me just about the whole of my career. Even when I was a boy boxing for the Repton Club, he was always there. He used to pack away all my equipment before and after those amateur fights, he was so careful you'd think he was handling the crown jewels!'

But Stracey was to learn that, while he might now be a world champion, the brand new sporting hero of all England, his father still had the last word. 'The fight was staged in the afternoon, so a group of us were in a restaurant about eight o'clock in the evening, having a celebration meal,' he said. 'I'd gone so far as to order a spaghetti bolognaise – that's way out for someone like me, who only ever ate plain, wholesome English food. Anyway, my father arrived just as they were serving me my meal. And he went spare. "You're not eating that foreign muck," he shouted. And he ordered the waiter to take it back – and bring me a steak instead. Here I was, champion of the world, but I still knew who the boss was!'

My Life is Chaos . . .
I Thrive on Chaos

Mike Tyson v Michael Spinks

Mike Tyson was born in Brooklyn, New York, on 30 June 1966. After failing to win a place in the American team for the 1984 Olympic Games in Los Angeles, he turned professional in 1985. On 22 November 1986 he knocked out Trevor Berbick to win the WBC world heavyweight title and become the youngest heavyweight champion in history – just 20 years, four months, 22 days old. By August of 1987 he had unified the crown, adding the WBA and IBF titles to his list. He lost all three titles to Buster Douglas in Tokyo in 1990 and was imprisoned for three years after being convicted of rape in 1992. He resumed boxing on his release and regained the WBC title in March 1996, stopping Frank Bruno in the third round in Las Vegas.

MIKE TYSON had an ominous message for those, Michael Spinks among them, who questioned whether the career of the world heavyweight champion was dangerously out of control. 'I thrive on chaos,' he answered. 'I've known nothing but chaos for most of my life. I've learned to lock it away when I'm fighting.' We are in the early summer of 1988 and, even by its own astonishing and disturbing standards, the life of Tyson, the self-proclaimed 'baddest man on the planet', is in turmoil. Spinks is the opponent – the most dangerous so far in the eyes of many – he must face at the Convention Center in Atlantic City, New Jersey, on 27 June in the richest contest in boxing's whole history. But Tyson seems, instead, to be at war with the rest of the world – and, perhaps most of all, with his own tortured mind. His life has become the stuff of dreams for the American tabloids. His wife of three months, the beautiful television actress Robin Givens, has claimed she is in fear of her husband's violent mood changes, that he has used his mighty fists on her. Allegedly pregnant when they married, she entered hospital after a 'miscarriage' just three weeks before his fight, although many doubted whether she had ever been carrying his child.

He was in the throes of acrimoniously severing his relationship with his manager Bill Cayton, who had helped to guide him on his all-conquering path through history. And lurking in the background was the controversial Don King, edging Tyson away from Cayton, plotting his own strategy to take promotional control of the most marketable property in the sporting world. Tyson, being tugged in three different directions, found his mind being twisted so savagely amidst the internal strife that the fight with Spinks became almost an irrelevance, even though it would earn him £14 million – the biggest fortune ever paid to a sportsman for a single event.

Tyson did not even begin serious training until barely a month before the contest. Even then his mind was filled with so many distractions that his trainer, Kevin Rooney, was locked in a constant battle to win his attention. There were few worries about the champion's physical fitness. This was, remarkably, his eighth world title fight in 19 barnstorming months, since he obliterated Trevor Berbick inside two rounds to win the WBC version of the title in November 1986. He was just 20 years old then, the youngest ever to win sport's supreme title. He had unified the crown by the following summer; his astonishing record of 34 straight victories in little more than three years – all bar four by knockout or stoppage – had already earned him near mythical status from a public enthralled by his terrifying ring presence and now absorbed by his highly publicised private life.

It was Tyson's mental state which caused the intrigue, though, as he prepared to defend his title against a challenger some claimed to be the true champion. Spinks, a distinguished world light-heavyweight champion, had moved up to capture the IBF heavyweight title from Larry Holmes in 1985. Holmes was generally considered to be the true champion at that time, so the mantle passed on to Spinks, an easy-going, mild-mannered man from St Louis who, at 31, was ten years Tyson's senior.

Spinks, also unbeaten in his 31 contests, had relinquished his title rather than take part in the elimination series which Tyson had wrapped up the previous year. That gave this particular fight an extra edge. Until Tyson overcame Spinks, he could not claim to be the supreme champion. It also served Spinks well, financially at least. His waiting game had finally earned him a challenger's purse of £8 million – more than three times the figure he would have earned for taking part in the earlier series as a champion.

Was Tyson emotionally prepared for the challenge? It was the all-consuming question as nearly 1,000 media workers from around the world gathered in America's decrepit and depressing East Coast gambling Mecca. Tyson gave his answer in an extraordinary interview reserved solely for the British press contingent, the only newspapermen he still trusted. Seated on the floor of his luxurious ocean-view apartment, his arms cradled round his wife, he said: 'Boxing and the rest of my life are two different compartments. Do I look like a guy in turmoil right now, three days before the fight? I'm relaxed and ready to go. I am the best fighter in the world. No one can beat me. Ever since I was 13 years old, I was groomed to be the world heavyweight champion. Cus [D'Amato, his former mentor] always used to drum into me that it would be like this, that I would have the kind of pressures I couldn't dream of. And he taught me how to cope with them.'

The fable of Cus, the crusty old boxing renegade who had taken on the Mafia back in the 1950s, and Tyson, the wild kid he plucked from reform school and moulded into a champion, is one of the most enduring in sporting legend. But it is somewhat over-simplified. Tyson was a product of the Brooklyn ghetto, a boy heading for prison or a bullet in his brain or a knife in his back before D'Amato's timely rescue. But the old man could never quite restrain the beast inside his protégé. He was often in trouble, even when Cus was alive. Then, following the death of D'Amato just a month before his world title success, and the equally sad loss of his co-manager Jim Jacobs five months before the fight with Spinks, Tyson had found himself without the guidance of the two men he looked up to, perhaps the only two men he ever truly trusted. Without them, and with so many other people now scrambling to take over the running of his life, it seemed the demons outside the ring were his most potent enemies. Yet that afternoon in his apartment he showed a man seemingly at peace with the world. He seemed more like a loving young husband on vacation than a champion preparing for his performance of licensed brutality. 'I'm in love with a beautiful woman. I'm young and I'm rich. But I'm still hungry,' he said. 'I want to go down in history as a great champion. That's why I have bad intentions in my mind right now. When I fight Michael Spinks, my objective is to inflict as much pain as possible. To win by a knockout.'

Spinks, meanwhile, had grown increasingly cautious as the fight approached. He talked about fear, declaring, 'It is a necessary part of a fighter's make-up. I will have fear inside me when I face Tyson – I always have that element of fear there with me.' It was an honest admission. But was it a signal that, like so many of Tyson's victims before him, the brutality of the man he was about to confront was beginning to strike terror into his heart even before a punch was thrown? Spinks's state of mind was hardly helped when he went to his dressing-room at the Convention Center to prepare. There was a sizeable hole in one of the walls, large enough to peer through and read the billboard across the street. 'How did that get there?' he asked, to be told that Tyson, who had occupied that room before he fought Larry Holmes at the arena in January that year, had thrown a left-hand combination at the wall – and smashed his right fist clean through!

Tyson had been cheered by meeting one of his boyhood idols, the legendary Roberto Duran, earlier in the day. Duran, whose own lust for battle inside the ring was matched by his wild living and big spending out of it, did not have a ticket for the fight and, in his current distressing financial state, could not afford to buy one. After their meeting, Tyson gave an aide $1,000 and told him to buy a ringside ticket for Duran. But if that was an example of the kind-hearted champion, Tyson was in a rage by the time he climbed into the ring. Butch Lewis, Spinks's manager, had caused a stir in Tyson's dressing-room less than an hour before complaining about a small lump in the bandaging on his hand. The officials were called and ruled that there was nothing untoward with it – but the interruption to his final preparations had made him mad. 'I just wanted to take it out on Michael Spinks. He's got his manager to blame,' Tyson said later. Now, clad in his normal gladiatorial attire – black shorts, black boots, no socks – he bounded out of his corner with all the urgency of a man in a fearful hurry.

Spinks had already looked increasingly apprehensive during the preliminaries. It was a common thread among Tyson opponents. While the ring was still bustling and crowded, they could appear composed, shadow-boxing in their corner, perhaps managing even a half-smile. But once that ring began to empty, once they looked across at the man-monster in the opposite corner, once the awful reality dawned that in a few seconds it would be them against HIM, brave men would become wide-eyed with terror.

Those eyes had been the giveaway for Spinks. They were quickly to be displaying pain as he was blasted by a four-punch combination that sent him staggering backwards and covering up inside the first ten seconds. In desperation Spinks tried to fight back, but his punches missed wildly. If Tyson had malice and mayhem on his mind, this was to be no wild streetfight. Even amid the storm he was creating, the champion remained icily cool. 'I never lose my concentration. I throw every punch with bad intentions, but with thought behind them as well,' he said later. Spinks tried to grab and hold Tyson, seeking safety inside his punching range. But there was to be no respite from the onslaught, and no reprieve. The champion was blocking all avenues of retreat. There was nowhere to run, nowhere to hide from his cold-eyed executioner.

With barely a minute gone the rangy 6ft 2in challenger – three inches taller than Tyson – had already been cut down to size. Now he was to fall to the canvas for the first time in his career, battered there by a ferocious left uppercut to his jaw and then a devastating right hook which bent his body double as he fell. He was up at the count of two and was able to nod to his corner that he was all right as referee Frank Cappuccino continued the mandatory eight count. But Spinks was already a forlorn figure. In a final gesture of futility he threw a swinging right hand that missed as Tyson moved back in. The momentum of the punch, though, carried Spinks's whole body with it. As he swung round, his head was momentarily left totally exposed. Tyson needed no further invitation. With that instinct that comes as second nature to a fighting machine like him, he drove in a pulverising right hook that landed flush on Spinks's jaw. It would have felled an ox. It was altogether too much for the challenger, who went crashing backwards, his head bouncing off the floor to add to the concussive power of the punch. Spinks lay there until the count reached four, his eyes open but his body unable to respond to his mind's orders. He tried to rise, only to stumble face-first into the ropes as referee Cappuccino's count reached ten. It was all over in 91 seconds, the fourth-quickest finish to a world heavyweight title fight in history.

Tyson had earned more than £150,000 a SECOND for his greatest and most overwhelming triumph. He held his arms outstretched, palms upwards, as he walked matter-of-factly back to his corner. 'I knew it would be quick, because when I looked over at him before the first bell I saw fear in his eyes,' said the champion. 'There's no fighter like me. I can beat anyone in the world.' Within 24 hours Tyson was to stun the sporting world by announcing his retirement. 'I had fun, but I don't want any of this bullshit any more. I don't like reading that my wife is a whore and that I'm an idiot. It's time to call it a day.'

As history knows, he changed his mind because, in brutally simple terms, boxing was all he knew. His wife and his manager would be gone before his next fight, his faithful trainer Rooney – the last link with D'Amato – would be ousted as well within a year. Tyson was well on the destructive path that would eventually take him to prison. But on this night of spine-chilling savagery he really was invincible inside that square jungle. If only the jungle outside had been as brutally straightforward.

Glasgow Belongs to Me

Jim Watt v Howard Davis

Jim Watt was born in Glasgow on 18 July 1948. He crowned a fine amateur career by winning the ABA lightweight title in 1968, but declined an invitation to compete in the Olympic Games that year, turning professional instead. He won the British and European lightweight titles before capturing the WBC world title in 1979, when he was 30 years old. He successfully defended the title four times before being dethroned two years later.

AS JIM WATT recalls, 'Nothing for the rest of your life can compare with that wonderful moment when the referee holds up your hand to signify that you have won a world title.' But if that moment is all about elation, a champion can achieve an even deeper sense of personal satisfaction and pride from defeating a challenger universally expected to plunder the title as his right. That was the situation the tough, abrasive but underrated Scot faced when he defended his WBC world lightweight crown against the brash, brilliant and unbeaten American Howard Davis at Ibrox Park, home of Glasgow Rangers, on 7 June 1980.

Davis had been the outstanding star in the all-conquering American Olympic boxing team of 1976, plundering a gold medal in Montreal and outshining even the likes of Sugar Ray Leonard and the Spinks brothers, Michael and Leon, to win the accolade of best boxer at the Games. Since then he had smoothly eased his way past all before him in 13 professional fights. While his record suggested he still lacked that precious asset called experience, his advisers felt he was more than ready to capture his first world title from a champion unheralded and virtually unknown in America. The 24-year-old challenger showed his own disdain for Watt as soon as he arrived in Glasgow, two weeks before the scheduled date, to complete his training. 'Jim Who?' he taunted him, bragging: 'I could still beat him with one hand tied behind my back – and smoking a cigarette at the same time. He can't beat me. I've known since I was 16 years old that I was ordained to be a world champion. I'm quicker than Watt and he can't hit hard enough to beat me. He'd have to cut off my legs.'

Watt, ironically, was nearly 500 miles away from his native city, tapering off his training in London while his upstart challenger was baiting the rest of Scotland. 'We only got together once or twice for press conferences, but I took all he was saying with a pinch of salt,' he recalls. 'I knew that most people agreed with his boast that he would win, but that didn't trouble me at all. I had watched him on video. And I felt his style suited me down to the ground. Not only could I beat him – I really believed I could beat him easily.'

Watt was well used to being written off by the world. Indeed, he had virtually consigned himself to the scrap heap just four years earlier. 'I was British champion but I felt I had missed the boat as far as anything higher was concerned,' he said. 'My career just seemed to be drifting. I never thought of retirement, but I felt my only future lay in small-hall and dinner-club shows.' In 1976 he split with his manager Jim Murray, who had been his father-figure and mentor since his amateur days, and joined forces with the most successful British manager of the time, Terry Lawless. It was a masterstroke. Lawless saw the enormous, untapped potential in a 27-year-old who had already been beaten seven times in 29 fights. 'He was THE manager at the time, so I had no hesitation in joining him when he asked me,' says Watt. 'I knew that his stable had the connections which would help to get me decent fights. But I think the most important thing he did was to build up my confidence.' Watt also reaped the benefits of training at Lawless's gym above the Royal Oak public house at Canning Town, in the heart of London's East End. There he was able to hone his skills, sparring with the array of top-class fighters who fought under the Lawless/Mickey Duff joint banner. Within a year he had become European champion and in 1979, before his joyous home-city supporters, he stopped Alfredo Pitalua of Colombia to win his world crown.

But despite two successful defences, the doubters continued their whispers. Was he really world class? Davis, the mandatory challenger, presented the quality of opposition he knew would enable him to give the clearest possible answer. 'People also thought that, just a month short of my 32nd birthday, I'd seen my best days,' he recalls. 'But age didn't bother me at all. I hadn't been in a dozen wars. And my experience was a vital advantage. I had already been in 13 15-round fights – and he'd only had 13 fights all told. He'd never been 15 rounds before. I knew he would get nervous if the fight went into the later stages. And my plan was to make him so tired he'd hardly be able to stand.' All the hype engendered by Davis's pre-fight bluster had been enough to crack even the stony hearts of some of Glasgow's bookmakers, who made the American the favourite in Watt's own city. 'I thought the bookies were mad. But it suited me in a way. I went into that ring as hungry as any challenger. And just as anxious to prove myself,' he said.

Watt was also a southpaw, which he knew would add further to his chances. Orthodox fighters, especially those still very much in the learning stage of their career, do not take easily to opponents who fight 'the wrong way round', leading with a right-handed jab. 'But I felt the most important thing was to establish myself as the man dictating the fight from the start, to keep him on the back foot,' he said. The champion went on to produce his battle plan to perfection in the ring. The swirling rain had not dampened the enthusiasm of nearly 30,000 of Watt's countrymen who now roared him on. He remained cautious amid the cauldron for the first two rounds, then gradually took control.

Davis, a flashy challenger with lightning fast hands, was slowly but relentlessly driven back, forced to operate a defensive campaign, just as Watt had schemed. 'It meant that most of his shots were out of range, they were stopping a couple of inches short of the target,' said Watt. But the champion was enjoying a much more fruitful haul with his sharp, stabbing punches. They were taking their toll on the American, who became increasingly desperate as the rounds passed by. Watt was never a flamboyant performer, but he was an astute tactician, who had learned how to avoid punches or lessen their impact by the merest turn of his body. He brought all that experience into play now, ensuring that Davis's flailing attacks gained little reward.

The challenger had climbed off the floor to win two of his previous contests – and that left Watt believing he could not only defeat him but stop him in the later rounds. 'But give him credit, he was a lot grittier than I had expected,' said Watt. He had to be as he endured remorseless punishment in the final stages. Some of Davis's punches did make their mark as well, however, and by the end both fighters had blood seeping from cuts around their left eyes. Cuts had often posed a problem for Watt, as they do for fighters with thin facial skin tissue. But he was able to shrug off any discomfort as he pounded his relentless way to a unanimous victory.

'It was a sweet moment because I wanted to prove to those who still questioned my ability that I was a genuine world champion, as good as any lightweight in the world,' recalls Watt, now a successful businessman in Glasgow and a greatly respected ringside expert analyst with ITV – his expertise and the bluff, Cockney banter of commentator Reg Gutteridge combine to produce a formidable team. 'I'd like to think that my winning a title after all those years is proof to any boxer that it's never too late to succeed in this game. And also never to be afraid of reputations – you're only fighting a guy who's made of flesh and blood, the same as you are, at the end of the day.'

Yank Who Stormed the Alamo

Pernell Whitaker v Julio Cesar Chavez

Pernell Whitaker was born in Norfolk, Virginia, on 2 January 1964. Always acknowledged as a boxer of consummate skills, he climaxed a brilliant amateur career by winning a gold medal at the Olympic Games in Los Angeles in 1984 and turned professional a few months later. He captured the IBF, WBC and WBA titles to become the undisputed lightweight champion of the world in 1990, then moved up to win the IBF world junior welterweight title in 1992. Within a year he had moved up a further division, capturing the WBA world welterweight title.

OLD LOU DUVA kept on repeating the message to anyone who cared to listen. 'Styles make fights – that's why Pernell Whitaker will beat Julio Cesar Chavez.' Not that too many bothered. The boxing circus had travelled to San Antonio, Texas, to witness a coronation. And it wasn't Whitaker's. His role in the proceedings was simply to hand over the WBC world welterweight crown to Chavez and help write a further chapter in the legend of the brilliant Mexican, already revered as the greatest pound for pound fighter in the world.

Chavez already boasted a record to stand among the greatest of all time – 87 fights, 87 thrilling victories. Only a dozen of those opponents had even managed to survive his relentless onslaught. He had already proved himself supreme among the world's junior lightweights, lightweights and junior welterweights, plundering titles in all three divisions. All told, he had fought his way triumphantly through 25 world title fights. At 31, the master blaster from Culiacan was already the idol of all Mexico. And he was only 13 fights away from creating his own unique mark in sporting history by reaching a perfect century. The boyish face concealed a mature, intelligent fighting brain to accompany his destructive powers. Chavez was a crafty fighter as well as a dynamic puncher. He was as adept at cutting off the ring, which means cutting an opponent's avenues of escape, as any boxer ever was.

Whitaker was a genuine opponent, no question about that. Since emerging from the 1984 Olympic Games in Los Angeles with a gold medal, he had also fought his way up through three divisions – lightweight, junior welterweight and then welterweight – to rival Chavez as a triple champion. He was two years younger than the Mexican and was also universally acclaimed as being among the top four or five boxers of the day. That's where the similarity ended. For in their styles, the pair were as opposite as day and night. If Chavez was the eternal warrior, Whitaker was the ultimate craftsman. He believed that power alone, even the phenomenal brand produced by Chavez, would always be overcome by blindingly quick reflexes, by mobility and by strategy. This was his way of fighting, and while it was a style that produced appreciative applause rather than edge-of-the-seat drama, it had certainly served him well – only one defeat on his 33-fight record, and that a hotly disputed one, was testimony to that. They might well have been the tactics Jim Bowie and Davy Crockett had employed at the Alamo, San Antonio's most famous landmark, some 150 years earlier. The Americans lost that heroic defence to Santa Ana's Mexican Army though. Whitaker, as he made his lonely way to the ring on the night of 10 September 1993, could have been forgiven for musing that nothing much had changed.

The Alamodome, the shiny new £120 million arena adjacent to the old mission fort, was packed to the rafters. Apart from a handful of friends and family, who had travelled from his home town, Norfolk, Virginia, to support Whitaker, the baying, screaming 56,959 crowd was made up almost entirely by Mexicans. Chavez, as the challenger, had entered the ring first to a welcome so uproarious it bordered on hysteria. Not since Santa Ana captured the Alamo more than a century earlier, it seemed, had so many Mexicans crossed the Rio Grande to support their supreme leader! A Mexican band at least a dozen strong had climbed into the ring to serenade his regal entrance. They remained there, still playing cheerfully as Chavez and his own huge entourage rumbled in alongside them. By the time Whitaker and his comparatively tiny team arrived, there was barely a square inch of space left. It was a scene of utter chaos, of wild emotions . . . yet the calmest man amid all the bedlam was the man defending his title.

'I wasn't at all frightened or overawed because I had trained my mind to expect it,' he said later. 'In fact, I wanted to hear them jeering me, especially when the fight was on. It meant I was making them nervous, that I was beating their man. I had no fear of Chavez's reputation because I always believed his come-forward style was made for a counter-puncher and a quick mover like me. I didn't just expect to win – I expected to win easy.'

Chavez, for his part, had poured scorn on Whitaker's elusive hit-and-run style, declaring: 'I hope he fights me like a man, not runs like a mouse.' If it was meant to unnerve Whitaker, it failed. 'I kept telling everybody that Whitaker's style would be too damn sharp for Chavez. Nobody listened. But I knew . . . and Pernell knew. He didn't have a trembling hair on his head,' said Lou Duva, Whitaker's veteran co-trainer, co-manager and cheerleader.

If Whitaker was unfazed, he was ultra-cautious as well for the opening couple of rounds, content to circle and move away from Chavez's early attacking sorties. Aggression alone won those rounds for the Mexican. It seemed the pattern for the contest was set. But Whitaker's chief trainer, George Benton, urged him to 'be more positive, start throwing your jab' in the break before round three. Benton, once close to being a world champion in his fighting days, is one of the shrewdest cornermen in the game. Whitaker took his advice. Suddenly Chavez found two, three, even four jabs pumping into his face every time he attempted to advance. And his opponent wasn't moving backwards any more. Instead, Whitaker was using those quicksilver reflexes to slip everything Chavez threw at him, catching him with hurtful counter-punches of his own, then tying him up inside. Chavez's temper began to boil over as the frustration rose inside him. He had already established a reputation for being, shall we say, careless with his punches in tough situations. In round five, he threw a left hand so low it caught Whitaker on the thigh. It has to be said that Whitaker was crouching so low at times it seemed his chin was touching the canvas. But the low punch from Chavez still incensed the American – and his corner.

'If he fights dirty, I'll fight back dirty,' Whitaker had warned. He was as brutal as his word – in the following round he smashed a left hook into Chavez's protective cup, leaving the Mexican writhing in agony. Referee Joe Cortez gave him 45 seconds to recover but, perhaps sensing that this was a classic case of the biter being bit, did not deduct a point from Whitaker. It was that kind of fight. Jungle warfare spiced with genius. By the end of that sixth round, the halfway stage, there was nothing to separate the two men.

From that stage on, though, Chavez must have felt like a man being blown away in a Texas dust-storm as Whitaker unleashed his full formidable repertoire. He was no longer the dancing cavalier. Now he was ready to stand toe to toe with Chavez, leaving the Mexican increasingly bemused by the speed and the venom of his punches. And driving him back – a sight we had never expected to witness from the macho king. The situation became so desperate for Chavez that, in the break before the 11th round, his cornermen lifted his three-year-old son Omar on to the apron in an effort to spur him on.

He did try, manfully, to catch up with his tormentor, but he was chasing a ghost. Even the huge crowd had grown silent as Whitaker continued his now-you-see-me-now-you-don't way to the final bell. The American corner was jubilant – this time they'd surely written a new ending to the second battle of the Alamo. Then the official result was announced – one judge had awarded it to Whitaker by two points but the two others had both scored the contest a draw. Under the majority verdict rule of the WBC, that meant the result was a draw . . . and a wretched miscarriage of justice.

Even his thousands of worshippers could raise little more than an embarrassed, bedraggled whimper of a cheer for Chavez, who compounded the injustice by claiming later that he should have won. 'Without me there was no fight. All he did was run,' he declared, the vivid bruising on his face giving its own lie to his testimony. Whitaker, to his credit, did not bleat about the travesty he had suffered. 'I know I won the fight. Julio knows I won the fight. And the rest of the world, the millions who watched it on television, they know I won the fight.' It was a statement that brooked no argument. Some days later, after time to reflect, he said: 'I waited two years for this fight. Chavez was always the guy I most wanted to fight. And it went more or less the way we planned it. I knew I would be moving too sweet for him. I didn't get the verdict, but I did dent his record. It can never be perfect again. And when people look at the draw after those 87 wins, they'll know it was Sweet P who put it there. And they'll remember that I won the fight, in reality.'

He might have added that his moral victory lifted him instantly on to the pedestal of being acknowledged in place of Chavez as the greatest fighter in the world. There can be no greater pinnacle for any man within his own sporting confines. But perhaps his most abiding boxing epitaph will be: The Man Who Buried the Legend of Julio Cesar Chavez.

Cruel Hand of Fate

Howard Winstone v Vincente Saldivar

Howard Winstone was born in the tough Welsh valley town of Merthyr Tydfil on 15 April 1939. He won all but three of his 86 contests in a brilliant amateur career that reached a triumphant finale in 1958, when he won the ABA title and then Wales's only gold medal in the Empire Games before his ecstatic followers in Cardiff. In an equally spectacular professional career he became British, European and finally world featherweight champion before retiring in 1968. He was a boxer of dazzling skills, but his most remarkable achievement was to fight at all after losing the tips of the fingers on his right hand when they were crushed by a power press in the toy factory where he worked. He was just 17 at the time.

WALES REJOICED when Howard Winstone finally put the seal on his magnificent career by capturing the WBC world featherweight title in 1968 with a ninth-round stoppage victory over Japanese Mitsunori Seki. It was a reign that would last only six months, before Winstone, long past his glorious prime, lost to the youthful challenge of Cuban Jose Legra. But at least it meant that the little maestro from Merthyr Tydfil, the uncrowned capital of the Welsh valleys, would be revered forever as a world champion. For until that night, it seemed that Winstone, for all his consummate skills, would be remembered instead as the man who had the greatest prize snatched cruelly from his grasp, as the man who won the fight but never got the verdict. 'It's funny, but more people talk about that fight I lost than any I won,' smiles Howard. 'I guess it was the most memorable night of my career. It was certainly my greatest fight.'

The contest he refers to – and one which will provoke an argument in any public bar in Wales right up to the present day – was the second in his gripping three-fight series against the tigerish Mexican, Vicente Saldivar. They were wars of attrition that enthralled the sporting fraternity on both sides of the Atlantic. Winstone, the purist, the matador of exquisite, quicksilver skills, against Saldivar, the raging Mexican bull who never took a backward step – and never stopped hurling that fusillade of punches from his southpaw stance.

The two vividly contrasting styles presented a match made in heaven. In their first and third meetings, Saldivar's brute strength was the dominant factor. He simply outgunned and outscored the Welshman at London's Earls Court on 7 September 1965, leaving neither Winstone – nor any of the packed 18,000 audience – with any argument. 'No complaints. I didn't know anything about his style until we got in the ring. And I could never settle – he never allowed me to,' admits Howard. 'He was the toughest man I ever met. But I knew that if I fought him again, it would be a different story. I'd learned all about him from that first fight. I would be ready for him next time.'

That next time was to come at Ninian Park, home of Cardiff City football club, two years later on 15 June 1967. Now Howard was ready to tame that bull. He had scored half a dozen convincing victories since the first encounter and he was at his absolute peak of fitness. He had baffled his sparring partners in training camp at Carmarthen with his breathtaking speed and sorcery. Now that cherished world title beckoned. 'I felt great. I even had most of my hair cut off – I used to have a Tony Curtis look, all wavy with long sideboards, but I felt it would be too hot in the ring for me in the middle of summer. So I went and had it all taken off. I guess it helped to make me look a bit tougher, more like a fighter,' he said. It certainly didn't take away his strength, in the way a famous haircut once did to an old-time fighter called Samson.

Winstone, greeted by a ferocious reception from his 25,000 supporters as he entered the ring, began his challenge with demonic speed and cunning. Saldivar continually bulldozed his way forward, never stopping with his barrage of punches, never willing to give ground. But he must have felt he was fighting The Invisible Man as those punches landed only in the night air. Winstone never stood still in front of him for a second, never gave him a target to aim for.

As the Mexican came lunging in, he would be picked off unerringly by the jabs peppering into his face.

By the tenth of the 15 rounds, Saldivar was beginning to look a sorrowful sight. Cuts had opened under both his eyes and his face was also bruised and swollen – painful testimony to Winstone's left hand which had ripped into him with such cruel purpose. By this stage, even the neutrals around the ringside had the Welshman well ahead. It seemed he had only to survive the last five rounds to emerge victorious. Saldivar sensed likewise. He knew his title was slipping away with every jab which thudded into his face. But now he displayed his own greatness as he summoned up a new reserve of strength borne of sheer desperation to claw his way back into the fight. Suddenly, as Winstone began to tire, the pattern of the contest changed. Now Saldivar's punches were starting to land on target, now it was Winstone being forced to cover up.

In the 14th round, with Winstone all but exhausted, he was finally trapped in a corner and driven to the floor by a two-fisted barrage. But he climbed back bravely to his feet and somehow managed to survive the storm that raged around him. 'I was more tired than I had ever been in my life,' he recalls. 'But I had worked so hard to get that title I wasn't going to let Saldivar or anyone else stop me now. When the bell went to end round 14, it was the sweetest sound I ever heard. I had a full minute to rest, then I had only to keep out of trouble for the last three minutes and, surely, the title would be mine. Give him credit, he had come back strong in the last few rounds, but I had to be still ahead after all the early rounds I won.'

That was the view shared by (nearly) everyone as Winstone called on all his remaining reservoirs of skill and fitness to keep Saldivar at bay and actually win the round through his clever counter-punching. Then came the bombshell that was to scar the brave challenger more than any punch from the champion ever could. In those days there were no judges to score fights in this country, even at world title level. The referee was the sole arbiter. Wally Thom, from Birkenhead, once a British welterweight champion himself, was the man in charge. Now, as a sudden hush descended on the stadium, Thom took a couple of steps towards Winstone's corner – then stopped, to re-examine his scorecard. Having done so, he abruptly turned round, walked towards Saldivar who had looked so crestfallen – and raised his hand.

The verdict was announced – and Thom had the champion ahead

by half a point, which meant he had retained his title by a single round. As the crowd screamed their fury, Winstone slumped in his corner, too exhausted to show any emotion, too tired even to cry. 'I was just numbed,' he said. 'I just couldn't comprehend it all. I'd done everything, given everything – and it still wasn't enough.' It was no consolation when even the victorious Saldivar told him: 'There should be two world champions. You did not deserve to lose this fight.'

Referee Thom had been involved in a well-known feud with Winstone's manager, another former British champion, Eddie Thomas. That led to dark mutterings throughout Wales that Thom had robbed Winstone in order to exact vengeance on Thomas. 'But I never believed that. Thom had his job to do and he did it,' says Winstone. 'I can't say I agree with him, but I still believe to this day that he acted honestly. I met him a few years later at a boxing function and we shook hands. The poor man's dead now – that shows that life's too short to hold grudges.

'But what I do believe – and I think the fight helped to prove it – is that it was just too much to expect one man to have to be the referee and the jury. It's hard enough for him having to keep two boxers in check. Thank goodness things have changed now and we have judges at all European and world title fights. At least when you have three people giving their result you're more likely to get the right one.'

Winstone fought Saldivar for a third time in Mexico City four months later. It was another titanic struggle, with Winstone again boxing his way to an early lead before finally being caught by the champion's barnstorming late rally. This time there was no need for a verdict. Manager Thomas threw in the towel to save his fighter in the 12th round as Winstone, his face a crimson mask of blood, sank to his knees under the onslaught. But Saldivar paid his own remarkable tribute to the vanquished challenger by announcing his retirement in his dressing-room immediately after the fight. 'I have no wish to ever endure pain like that again,' he told his startled followers.

After their bloody, brutal warfare, the two fighters became good friends, in the heroic tradition of boxing. 'I went out to stay at his home for three weeks, during the Olympic Games in Mexico in 1968. We had a great old time out there,' said Howard. 'And the best memory of all was when he told me quietly one night: "You did beat me in Cardiff. You were the better man that night." That meant more to me than anything.

'I was gutted when Saldivar died from a heart attack back in 1985. He was a great fighter, one of the world's best featherweights of all time. To have had three fantastic fights with him is a special memory that will always live with me. Even if I'll always believe that I beat him at least once out of the three!'